Earth Under My Heel

A journal of a walk across Northern Spain on the Camino de Santiago

– DAVID LITTLEJOHN BEVERIDGE –

An environmentally friendly book printed and bound in England by
www.printondemand-worldwide.com

Mixed Sources
Product group from well-managed
forests, and other controlled sources
www.fsc.org Cert no. TT-COC-002641
FSC © 1996 Forest Stewardship Council

PEFC
PEFC/16-33-415

PEFC Certified
This product is
from sustainably
managed forests
and controlled
sources
www.pefc.org

This book is made entirely of chain-of-custody materials

i

www.fast-print.net/store.php

EARTH UNDER MY HEEL
Copyright © David Littlejohn Beveridge 2014

A catalogue record for this book is available from the British Library

ISBN 978-178456-063-8

First published 2014 by
FASTPRINT PUBLISHING
Peterborough, England.

This book is dedicated to my
ever expanding family

www.waterunderthekeel.co.uk

To

My dear friends Ida & Clive

with kind regards from

David Littlejohn Beaumont

3ʳᵈ December 2014

ACKNOWLEDGMENTS

I could not have produced this little book without the support and tremendous work of my wife Patsy. While I was on the camino she faithfully plotted my progress on the maps which she set up, like an operations room, in our dining room. Each day the caterpillar red line of my journey was faithfully recorded, and each day she took my brief and sketchy reports and turned them into interesting bulletins for our family, amplified and adorned by the details she had discovered about the country I passed through. This labour would later prove invaluable when I came to write this book, because the forensic work she did over many weeks in identifying buildings, places and events which I had not taken note of, enabled me to put the photographic images into order, an impossible task without her efforts. Not only this, she reconciled the time disparity between the three cameras which were used to record events, for I had omitted to synchronise them. All in all it was a Herculean task. Her advice in the selection of images was also invaluable.

My son Joseph who accompanied me from Roncesvalles to Burgos, not only took a huge number of photographs, indeed all the best images are his, but was the very spirit of generosity during his time with me, for he saw me want for nothing. He is a great companion and a stalwart friend.

I am indebted to John Brierley for his book *A pilgrims guide to the Camino de Santiago*. It is an outstanding work from every point of view and I have no hesitation in recommending it to any prospective pilgrim.

I would like to thank the Confraternity of St. James not only for providing good practical advice for the journey but also for permitting me to use an image of their *Pilgrim's Record* which appears on the rear cover. The Refugio Gaucelmo at Rabanal, which they own and operate, is a delight, and the memory of it marks one of the high points of my own pilgrimage.

Lastly I would like to thank each and every fellow pilgrim I encountered on the road. Without exception, they have enriched my life in ways I cannot number and they will continue to travel with me for the rest of my days.

EARTH UNDER MY HEEL

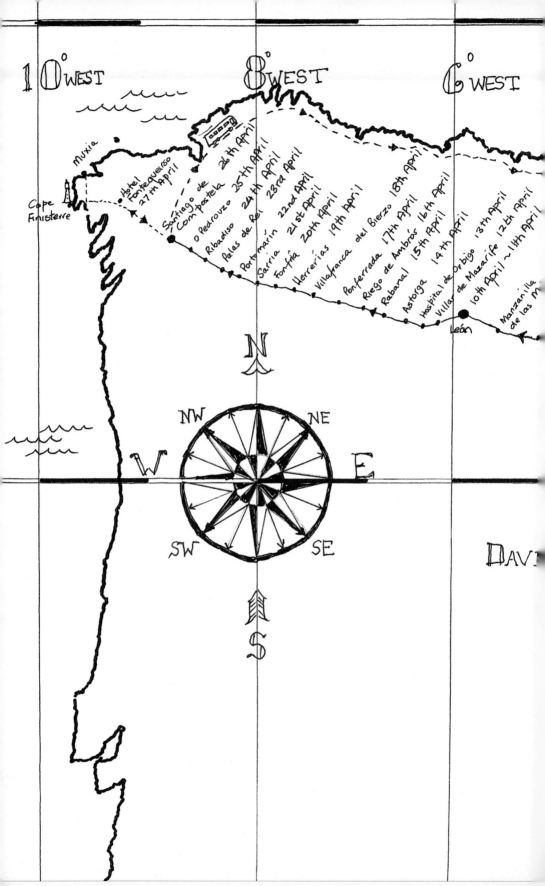

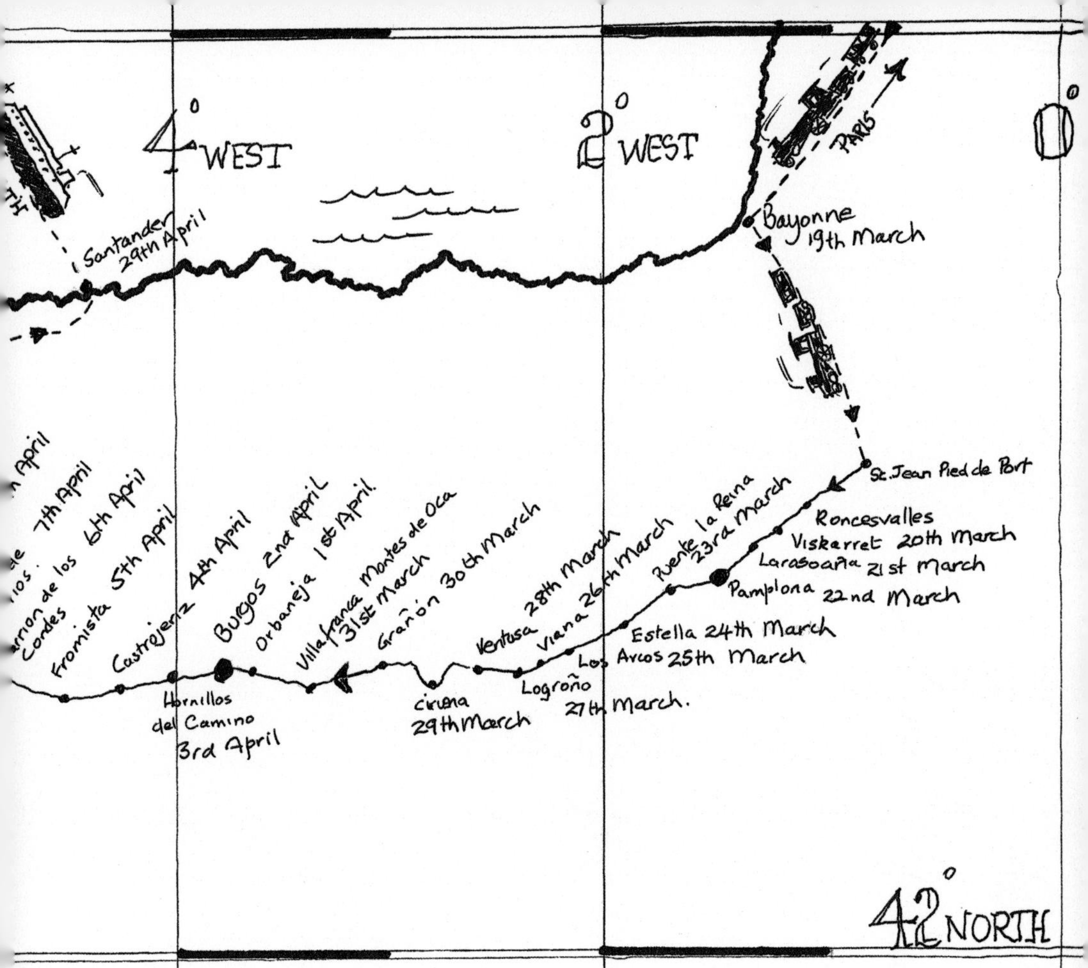

4° WEST   2° WEST   0°

PARIS

Bayonne
19th March

Santander
29th April

St. Jean Pied de Port

Roncesvalles
Viskarret 20th March
Larasoaña 21st March
Pamplona 22nd March

Puente la Reina
23rd March

Viana 26th March

28th March

Estella 24th March
Los Arcos 25th March

Logroño
27th March.

7th April
..rion de los 6th April
Cordes
Fromista 5th April

Castrojeriz 4th April

Burgos 2nd April

Orbaneja 1st April

Villafranca Montes de Oca
31st March

Grañón 30th March

Ventosa

Ciruña
29th March

Hornillos
del Camino
3rd April

42° NORTH

EVERIDGE'S CAMINO DE SANTIAGO
2013

Introduction

Two books, I now realise, as I lumber reluctantly through the autumn of my life, have influenced me significantly. The one, *The Prologue to Chaucer's Canterbury Tales* and the other *The White Company* by Sir Arthur Conan Doyle. They appeared on my twelve year old horizon at a pivotal moment and quietly, subconsciously, without fanfare, slipped into my adolescent mind, wooing me into a love affair with the romance of the Medieval Period. Of course, I now realise that this romantic era never actually existed as a golden age of chivalry, but the myth, which would give birth to so many books, paintings, poems and dreams is as alive today as it always has been, for like all ideals it relies for its life on the good aspirations, existing as shadows, that men dream about and seldom attain.

The transitional English of Chaucer thrilled me. I could feel the latent power of the words birthing into the language I would come to regard as the pinnacle of linguistic excellence. The most adaptable and vibrant living vehicle of ideas, emotions and aspirations on the planet. In this reverie of discovery I was willing to join Chaucer on his pilgrimage and so the notion of someday embarking on a similar enterprise was born.

Running concurrently with this discovery, *The White Company* took me on a journey from England to France and Spain where I fought the French in the company of the sturdy bowmen Sam Aylward and John Hordle, gained my imaginary "spurs" alongside Alleyne Edricson with whom I was able empathise so easily, since my surname apparently, like his, was Anglo-Saxon in origin. Eventually these notions would be tucked away in the bottom drawer of my memory and would only re-surface when the mental liberty afforded by retirement drew them into the daylight and presented them afresh to my superannuated mind.

Pilgrimage was big in medieval times. The doctrine of "Purgatory", that intermediate state where the "not quite righteous enough dead" are held until sufficient suffering had been endured and sufficient prayers had been offered, ensured that would be the case. The belief that time in this quasi hell might be reduced by doing good works to gain favour and therefore remission, was (and I suppose in some quarters, still is) a strong one. Donations to the church, almsgiving and a host of other favour-winning activities were undertaken, and travelling from one's home to holy sites such as Jerusalem, Rome, Santiago, Canterbury and Walsingham, in the hope that the pilgrim would somehow be imbued with the goodness of whichever saint's shrine was visited, developed as a powerful means of obtaining favour with God. Treks of this kind would be long, arduous, dangerous, and potentially life-threatening; tens of thousands of people over the last thousand years or so have made such a journey.

For my own part there were no such ideas in my mind. I long ago realised that if my salvation was hung upon the shaky peg of my own puny efforts at self-improvement, then my condition was perilous indeed. I recall it was with a joy akin to that of Luther himself, when I comprehended at last that it was not by my wretched labours but by faith in the perfect, finished, atoning, work of Jesus Christ who shed His blood on the cross of Calvary for sinners like me that I would enter the gates of heaven.

Nothing has caused me, after all these years, to alter my belief in the slightest.

That said, I acknowledge there is something gloriously romantic and testing about going on a pilgrimage. Like a personal Grail quest, it is an opportunity to free the mind and soul of the daily cares and challenges of normal life, for one is simply too far away to influence anything that is happening away from the immediate vicinity, and the only effect one can have is through the communication afforded by the uniquely versatile iPhone. I took an iPhone with me at my wife's insistence for she feared, and so did I, that I might fall ill when alone and at least I could summon help.

The responsibilities of "normal life" are nowhere to be found on the road, and instead the pilgrim's life becomes simplified into preserving the body for daily physical work, finding food and shelter and interacting with those he meets on the road. With such an absence of distractions, the soul is indeed more able to contemplate not only its own condition but also to grasp a wider view of all of life and perhaps glimpse hazy visions of the eternal.

Things which are usually deemed "important" are set in a new context and the priorities which lash and importune the modern mind, disintegrate, evaporate and dissipate in the persistent padding of boots upon the trail.

My pilgrimage on the Camino de Santiago has been and continues to be a profoundly significant event in my life, so much so that I am emboldened to record what took place each day, for I kept a journal which I completed as faithfully as any ship's log. It is my hope that any reader might be encouraged to do as I did and become a pilgrim.

Preparations & Equipment

There are several areas, I believe, in which the aspiring pilgrim has to do some thinking and work before embarking on his journey. I will tell you what I did and you can decide for yourself if what I did is of use to you.

I realised early on that my feet and my general physical condition would be paramount if my trip was to be successful. Thankfully, I enjoy fairly robust health, high blood pressure and the odd episode of atrial fibrillation notwithstanding. Nevertheless from autumn 2012 I started going for walks of ever increasing length, exploring on foot the area around my home in South Lanarkshire, with a seven to ten kilogramme rucksack on my back,. This was a superb preparation for the Camino for I would discover that often the terrain would be very similar. This slow incremental approach gradually built my stamina and strength and by the time I came to leave for Spain around the middle of March I could comfortably walk for twenty kilometres, which I had set as a personal maximum for a day's work. This turned out to be good for me as I often met much younger people on the road who pushed themselves too far and had to take days off to heal their feet and legs. I noted on these training walks, which were executed over the winter, that water was important for the wellbeing of the whole metabolism. Of course I knew and had heard this said many times but to discover the fact with regard to my own body was a useful revelation.

When it came to choosing my footwear I had no difficulty, for having worn Clark's shoes and boots for long periods of my life I knew that their lasts were, and continue to be perfect for my feet. I describe my feet as "biblical" to my wife, alluding to the paintings which one used to see in family Bibles. Invariably Abraham and other patriarchs were drawn with chunky square feet not dissimilar to my own, hence the name. Be that as it may, it would be Clark's hiking boots for me retailing at about £99.00 on the internet. With their Gore-Tex lining, wide fit and leather uppers I can say without exaggeration that they were outstanding. I did not suffer from blisters at all except on one occasion, through no fault of the boots, when the camber of the road drove my foot constantly to one side for many kilometres. That wonderful invention to deal with blisters which is marketed as Compeed was easily able to cope with that. Despite many downpours and often deep, muddy puddles, especially in the Rioja region where the red mud clings with unbelievable tenacity, I never once experienced wet feet – not even damp! At the end of each day I would marvel at how odour-free both feet and boots were, which could not be said for some of my fellow pilgrims! I substituted the laces which came with the boots as soon as I received them with heavy duty climbing boot laces as they did not look sturdy enough.

I took a pair of sandals for use at night.

Allied to my boots were my socks made by Bridgedale. For some years now I have taken to wearing Bridgedale Summit Knee High socks throughout the year except on the hottest days. They are wonderfully cushioned and formed to the foot so that there are never any hard ridges to create blisters. They are warm yet breathable ensuring the lower legs are always comfortable, with superb support for my varicose veins. Under the heavy socks I always wore a thin inner sock by either Bridgedale or Mountain Warehouse. I took three pairs of each.

I took three sets of vests and underpants made by Marks and Spencer. They were advertised as being less prone to bad odours and they certainly lived up to the claim. They also dried quickly.

In Mountain Warehouse I purchased two merino wool base layers which would be the only shirts I would have. They were warm or cool as required, which I thought was a truly amazing achievement. They also dried fairly quickly and again resisted bad odours.

Also in Mountain Warehouse, I bought a pair of windproof/showerproof trousers. These were very comfortable and when supplemented by my Isotex waterproof trousers rendered me bomb proof, although for long periods I sported an old pair of knee length trousers, worn like old-fashioned climbing breeks with my socks. In heavy mud I wore Gore-Tex gaiters from Tiso over the socks.

For an outer shell for bad weather I purchased a Berghaus Mera Peak jacket, again with Gore-Tex lining. This is a time honoured piece of equipment which needs no recommendation from me. It is an excellent garment.

For extra warmth on very cold days I took a good quality fleece which I had been given by a ship-repair company in Hull when I took my ship there to dry-dock.

That was all the clothing I had.

I had originally intended to camp on the Camino, and took with me a brand new Vango Helium one man tent, Vango lightweight stove, cooking gear, Thermalite sleeping mat, and other bits and pieces including a recharging system for the iPhone battery. This would all be sent home from Pamplona.

My sleeping bag was a 1.6 kilogramme microfiber filled type which was all I needed for the conditions I encountered, being every night in some lodging or another. I also had a silk sleeping bag liner, which would increase the thermal efficiency of my bag by 2 degrees centigrade if required. I never had to use it.

Besides this I took gloves, which at times I was profoundly grateful for, and indeed I bought a woollen hat and a sky blue poncho cape in Castrojeriz, so intense was the cold rain on the wind at times.

I carried a head lamp which was invaluable, not only for groping about in albergues (hostels) but also out on the trail in dark mornings.

I took my walking stick which I made about twenty years ago from a deer's antler and a fine straight piece of birch. This proved a great favourite amongst the local men all along the trail, who are great hunters and saw the attractiveness of it. Much later in the trip I bought another walking pole to balance my old stick for I had a tendency to walk lopsided with just one stick. You find these things out when you walk a long way.

A toilet bag, with my medication and a bar of the Spanish equivalent of Sunlight soap, which I had not seen for many a long day completed my equipment. This soap doubled as shampoo and clothes washing soap for I did all my washing by hand. I took one of the new lightweight towels to dry myself.

All of this was carried in a 75 litre rucksack I bought in Tesco a few years ago for no particular reason.

I have found by painful experience that the pilgrim's greatest enemy is weight, so much so that if I should impart only one piece of learned wisdom it is *keep weight to a minimum!* I have always been prone to carrying too much gear, having done most of my walking and camping in the mountains of Scotland where it is still possible to encounter wilderness conditions with four seasons in one day. The Camino is not like that. There are very few places where it feels right to camp, and the Way is more than adequately served by hostels, hotels and lodgings of several species. Food is also easily obtainable every few miles except at siesta time, and even then one can usually find a bar or café. It is important to take water along each day and I found that two half litre bottles were better than a big litre bottle. I am not a fan of the water bags with the tube unless one can sterilise them from time to time. My walk was made from the middle of March to the end of April so it was never too hot, but I believe that it could be oppressively hot in summer, when water would be crucial.

Support

Some guide books advise leaving the mobile phone and camera at home. I can understand this, and if I did not have a wife and large family I would have, but I feel that it is just too much to ask loved ones to go for days, perhaps weeks, without word from the pilgrim, so I took both.

With the iPhone I was able to send home brief reports, scant offerings which my wife Patsy, who, having clearly missed her calling as a communications guru, would embed in interesting and amusing emails to our offspring. She would take these succinct signals, research the area I had covered, then send out much fuller and colourful progress reports, full of detail and "in-house" humour to our family and friends. They actually began to look forward to them and quizzed her if she missed a couple of days. In this way I felt slightly less selfish for throwing over my normal responsibilities.

I am an indifferent cameraman at best so if I ever do another pilgrimage I will leave the camera and just snap away with the iPhone. I found it more than sufficient, and I am now delighted to be able to share with others the images I obtained, when they politely feign interest.

For a guidebook I took John Brierley's *Camino de Santiago*. I found this an excellent aid in all respects, allowing me to plan my day's work and anticipate both the challenges and the delights which lay ahead. It is an outstanding work and very easy to read.

Administration

Before I went on the Camino I visited the doctor and told him what I intended to do. He sounded me out, took blood tests and advised me not to start by climbing the snow-covered Pyrenees. This was good advice and I took it. The week before we arrived, one poor soul died on the trail trying to get to Roncesvalles from St. Jean Pied de Port. For this reason I arranged for a car to convey my son Joe, who would accompany me for the first fortnight, and me, from St. Jean Pied de Port to Roncesvalles. I set this up over the internet and it was carried out efficiently by confirmatory mobile phone texts as the pick- up time approached.

I did not book any accommodation whatsoever, in order to enjoy the uncertainty of not knowing where I was going to spend the night.

I resolved not to travel by aeroplane because they disconnect one from the earth. I know they are essential for almost everyone but I preferred the overland or maritime methods of transport as I was not time-constrained.

I joined, and arranged for my son Joe to join the Confraternity of St. James. This is not essential but it was nice to contribute to the on-going work of raising the profile of the Camino de Santiago.

The following documents are essential:

A valid passport. (It is strange how easily the expiry date creeps up.)

A valid European Health Insurance Card (Assuming you are a citizen of an EU country.)

Travel Insurance. I think this is an essential when things seem to go missing so frequently.

A pilgrim passport or *credencial* This can be obtained either from a confraternity or a pilgrim/tourist office at the start of your walk.

The Journey

Monday 18th March 2013

Yesterday I became 64 years of age and today I am setting out with my son Joseph to walk across Spain on the Camino de Santiago. Joe will accompany me for about fourteen days then return to the Philippines where he is managing the refurbishment of a power station...

Patsy, my longsuffering and lovely wife, managed to organise us into leaving the house at 2130 to catch the local train to Central Station in Glasgow. It snowed as we made our way down to Cambuslang station and my imagination briefly bore me away to the Pyrenees where I could envisage conditions over the high passes. Conditions not to be taken lightly, I say, by a man of mature years with a tendency to flip into atrial fibrillation.

We thought we could board 2 hours before departure but were told by a helpful railway employee we could not, so we had a seat in the Arrol Lounge and Joe as usual bought the refreshments. I say "as usual", for herein Joe set a precedent for our journey which would continue till he left me in Burgos a fortnight later. He was more than generous to me. Patsy eventually did a reconnaissance, which she excels at, and discovered we could board sure enough at 2215. Patsy, Jenny our number two surviving daughter, and Martin our number three son, saw us safely on board and then went home, any melancholy being dispelled by the excitement of the prospect of the journey. We left on time at 2340, whereupon Joe and I repaired to the lounge for a night-cap of white wine and revelled in the prospect of adventure until the back of midnight.

Our cabin is Formica, clinically clean with stiff sheets, which must be wrenched from their moorings under the mattress and which scuff reassuringly against our pyjama-clad legs as we slip into our bunks. Joe is in the top bunk in deference to my new-found old age. As we rumble with pneumatically cushioned ease over the points at some lonely halt, my mind drifts back to another sleeper car over sixty years ago, and I become a child again as I remember a similar excitement and prospect for adventure as I sped south with my parents to London from Aberdeen. I drift into sleep remembering the ghosts of long dead railway stewards, coal smoke and steam and the "tickety tick" of the rail-track under the iron wheels.

Tuesday 19th March 2013

I slept very well, only being disturbed when Joe used the facilities at 0245. We both then slept till about 0600. The train was running a bit late, but we received our tea at 0645 which was most acceptable. Some things never change, especially morning tea on the sleeper from the north. It is reassuringly British in taste and consistency, although the "Digestive" biscuit now comes Cellophane wrapped.

We were off the train by 0745 and on our way to St.Pancras where we arrived around 0815 for breakfast, consisting of rolls filled with bacon, egg and sausage. Joe reckoned the sausages were made of mushrooms – "or some other protein constituent". I was unable to comment on this having never been shipmates with mushroom sausages before so I just ate them acknowledging they might be a bit *foosty* (Scots word meaning stale). We set off on time from St. Pancras after a painless transit through check-in. The "Eurostar" from St. Pancras is fast and pleasant, clean and modern with exciting colours to gladden the heart of the most world weary traveller. Soon after leaving London the train dives underground, under the English Channel to surface in France.

Cambuslang Station - 18th March

Sleeper to London -18th March

Joe in Bayonne at night - 19th

Bayonne Cathedral – altar-20th March

Pilgrim Office at Roncesvalles Monastery - 20th March

The remnants of the huge snow drifts at Roncesvalles Monastery -20th March

Beginning of the long trek -20th March

The snowy path leaving Roncesvalles -20th March

Viskaret our first overnight stop - 20th March

It is low-lying, undulating countryside dotted with unobtrusive farms, wind turbines and pylons. Snow clings to the verges and under hedgerows. A last hurrah of winter we hope. The sun breaks out from behind lumbering, towering cumulous clouds and we enjoy the effortless journey to Paris. I am concerned about the transit from Gare du Nord to Gare Montparnasse; unnecessarily, for the Metro is excellent and thanks to good advice on the internet and good signage we arrive on time at Montparnasse. We eat an exotic sandwich called *poules villageois* which is tasty and fills a void very well. Ere long our next train is due and we make our way along its huge length – it turns out to be two trains and we must be careful to choose the right one. We do. After about one and a half hours we pass through Poitiers at 80 miles per hour. It is gone in an impression of light coloured buildings ranged on the side of a hill overlooking a river. I muse about English and Welsh archers trouncing the French cavalry. The halfway mark of the long journey is around Bordeaux. The countryside here is defined by its flat nature with few undulations. The other feature is unbroken tracts of pine trees which appear to be about twenty years old all the way from Bordeaux to Dax. I think they may have been planted to prevent erosion – perhaps not.

We arrived at Bayonne and disembarked around 1940. We were immediately filled with the excitement of being in a foreign place. It looked and smelled different and as the darkness fell it took on a delightfully exotic air. We found a pleasant wee hotel near the station called "Côtes de Basque". The internal walls had been removed of plaster and painted white giving the room a rusticated finish somewhat at odds with the general ambience of the building itself. Once we were established in the hotel with our gear stowed away nicely we sought out a chic looking restaurant, the cuisine of which was outstanding. Joe paid. The food and drink mellowed us so that we ambled in a light headed fashion as we made our way back to the hotel for a shower then turn in.

Wednesday 20th March 2013

We slept very well although from time to time we could hear people outside even at three in the morning when Joe rose to use the facilities. (I was beginning to worry about his bladder, then realised that he drinks prodigious amounts of water throughout the day which must go somewhere!) Our breakfast was very Continental – not a sausage, even of the mushroom variety, in sight! With some time to kill till our train at 1048, we roamed around Bayonne, visiting the cathedral and another church called Saint Esprit. Both were wonderful, being ancient and full of character and mystery, bathed in deep shadows shot through by the light of the wonderful stain glass windows, which drew the eyes heavenward. It was a fitting commencement to our journey and set the tenor for how we would approach every town and village along the Way, for whenever we could we visited the local church.

Our train to Saint Jean Pied de Port was virtually brand new with plenty of leg room. Magnificent mountain scenery interspersed with old alpine-style houses appeared all round us, presenting enticing camera shots which Joe ably recorded until we arrived at Saint Jean Pied de Port at around 1220. There we were met by the very attractive Caroline Aphessteche who drove us through beautiful mountain scenery via hairpin bends the like of which we had never seen.

By 1300 we had arrived at Roncesvalles, where my friends of the White Company had ended their journey. There we had our *credenciales* logged in, and were able to visit the church. I prayed that God would accompany us every step of the way and share with us in the pleasure of the adventure. This was followed by a very pleasant meal in the restaurant in Roncesvalles. Joe had *polo* (pork) and I had soup and trout (*trucha*). We then started our Camino at about 1400 with a photograph beside the road-sign telling us we were only 790 kilometres from Santiago! The way was well marked and soon led us into woods where the snow lay very deep, so much so that we had to take to the N135 road. I actually fell into a drift as we did this and had great difficulty extricating myself. As soon as we could we returned to the Camino which led us though Burguete, Espinal, and eventually to Viskaret where we stopped for the night. The village was deserted and we walked around in that forlorn, aimless way that all strangers do. We had the place to ourselves and it was extraordinary that the only person we should meet was the sister of the owner of the *casa rural* we would stay in. She let us in and arranged our accommodation for 30 euros for the two of us. That night we bought food in the *supermercado* which consisted of two small rooms lined with shelves of victuals, so we bought two pizzas, sardines, chorizo, bread and beer, and Joe made a feast in the kitchen. Around 1930 the owner returned from Pamplona. She put on the central heating, made up the fire in the lounge and life assumed a rosy tinge; it was wonderful! Joe was weary and turned in about ten o'clock but I remained in the lounge simply enjoying the ambience of fire, peace, a glass of beer and a chance to take stock. I was actually in Spain with my middle son, embarked on an enterprise which had flitted in and out of the recesses of my mind for as long as I could remember. I was deeply grateful to God who had permitted me to get here, for so many things could have prevented me throughout a life which had experienced more than its fair share of exciting moments. I prayed out of thankfulness and thought of Patsy at home and all my sons, daughters and grandchildren. The lines had truly fallen to me in pleasant places. I slept very well.

Thursday 21st March 2013

We set off from Viskaret at 0820 and made a pleasant walk through Linzoain, Paso do Roldan, via Alto de Erro. It was a most beautiful day with the sun shining the whole time. The views were spectacular in the clear, clean air; the mountains in the distance covered in snow, the path leading us through woodlands with several steep inclines and descents. We took coffee in Zubiri. Such coffee! Joe would constantly wax lyrical about the coffee and quite rightly, for it is excellent even when decaffeinated or *descafeinado*. We then pressed on for Larrasoaña where we booked into a *pensión* called "El Peregrino". It is very pleasant, with pleasant décor, a pleasant shower, and a pleasant wee garden gnome who runs it with his wife as owners. She is also pleasant.

We met up with some other pilgrims when we went into a tavern to replace lost body fluids. They were a Belgian girl a retired lawyer from Lossiemouth, a young American from Washington DC, two Spanish lads and a lady market gardener from Germany. Where else in the world would one come across such a league of nations? All were open and full of the desire to reach out and discuss enthusiastically our shared goal of reaching Santiago, and not for the first time in my life I ask myself "whence come wars?" when my fellow human beings are so friendly. Joe took a picture in the hostelry, which incidentally was decorated with witches, showing a man with a white beard in the company of a dog, sitting at a table before a fire. It is a good picture and I will paint it some-day. The man is me.

Zubiri – 21st March

Approaching Larasoaña - 21st March

Dog and Man - 21st March

Passing Pamplona's old city walls - 22nd March

The Albergue Casa I Barola -22nd March

The Crucifixion procession Pamplona Cathedral -22nd March

Sustenance after two and a half hours
in the Cathedral – 22nd March

Friday 22nd March 2013

We departed Larrasoaña at 0800 after a breakfast of croissants and tea (coffee for Joe) in a small shop called "SHOP". The walk was most enjoyable, passing through Akerreta, Zurláin, Irotz, Zabaidica, Parque, Trinidad de Arre, then on through the outskirts of Pamplona till we arrived via the imposing gates of the old fortifications. The path, in the main, passed through delightful countryside sprinkled with rustic dwellings of great antiquity. There are many modern buildings which ape the style of the old houses, but they lack the genuine look. The doors are a study in themselves, for there are never two the same; the lintels fashioned out great oaks or chestnut trees and the verandas unpainted for generations yet still sound and solid, bearing testimony to the skill and artistic sensitivity of the builders.

We chose the first albergue we came to on entering the city. It is called Casa I Barola and was built last year. It is clean and purpose-built and quite adequate for communal living. The bunks would remind you of the berths in a fishing boat and I felt very at home. The showers were hot, after which Joe and I put all the equipment we did not think we would need into a box which Igno, the warden of the albergue, obtained for us. We then took it to the Post Office (*Correos*) and sent it home, all 8 kilogrammes of it! It should make our walking much easier for my shoulders were beginning to protest, and Joe's boots were not the best type for this kind of trail. After that we found an Italian restaurant called "La Tagliatelli" and had delicious pizzas. It was lovely day. That night we went to Pamplona cathedral to take part in the Rosary. It turned out to be a very big celebration, for the Rosary was only the beginning; a prelude to a Mass, followed by Stations of the Cross. Two and a half hours later we came out of the church! It was a huge undertaking and they carried around enormous "floats" with a statue of the Virgin, heavily bedecked in candles wearing a very ornate cloak which streamed behind, adorned with bright jewels on an indigo background resembling the starry host of heaven. There was also a float of the crucified Christ similarly lit. These floats were carried by 28 men dressed in surcoats and all hooded. It was almost intimidating. The men are controlled by a leader with a hammer with which he raps out the signals on the great carrying staves of the float. One strike to get ready, two strikes to lift, another strike to advance then all set off in time with a pronounced swaying gait, reminiscent of a sailor who has just walked ashore after a week of bad weather at sea.

After this lengthy service we repaired to a hostelry and discussed what we had seen. Joe rightly pointed out that this was a kind of visual aid which was probably started to add realism to an already powerful story but my mind always takes me back to the prophet Isaiah and his scathing account of how men chop down a tree, use some wood to warm themselves then fashion an idol to worship. I am not saying the folk were worshipping idols, I am just saying I am uncomfortable with the possibility of being wooed into doing so.

Saturday 23rd March 2013

We rose at 0700 and were away by 0800 taking a breakfast consisting of croissants and coffee in a little taberna then began our longest walk so far this trip. Through Pamplona then continuing southwesterly on a rising gradient through Zariquegui, where we lunched briefly on baguettes and ham, *bocadillos de jamón serrano* which Joe swears by. From there our path led over Alto del Perdon at 790 metres. Well named for it was a long slog to the wind-turbine covered ridge. At the top we took photographs

Alto del Perdon – 23rd March

Puente La Reina – 23rd March

Exploring Puente La Reina – 23rd March

Leaving Albergue Jakue in Puente La Reina – 24th March

beside a steel sculpture depicting pilgrims. Then downhill on a very stony path which wrought havoc on our feet, to Utrega and Obanos which small villages are becoming more populous with the building of new houses. Our last village that day was Puente la Reina. We booked into an albergue called Jakue. It is ideal with two iron bunk-beds in our private room. After cleaning up we walked round the village which was really picturesque and beautiful. As we wandered around the ancient buildings which had hosted and healed literally thousands upon thousands of pilgrims, quite by chance we spied our friends from the other day through the window in the Monastery albergue. They were doing sterling service to the pilgrim meal they had been supplied with. We then returned to Jakue and had a huge meal from the buffet, bringing a fitting conclusion to a truly wonderful but very tiring day.

Sunday 24th March 2013

Setting off at 0810 from Jakue albergue we met the lovely Belgian girl (we will call her Amélie) with whom we had walked many kilometres, waiting for us to go to the church, but there was no service. She then accompanied us all the day to Estella via Cirauqui, Lorca and Villatuerta. The scenery and weather were fantastic so much so that Joe, moved to record the beauty of Cirauqui in the distance framed by an olive tree, took a picture which would become the first scene I would paint when I returned home. At around 1200, in Cirauqui, we met up with other pilgrims and enjoyed an impromptu lunch. Everyone was so amiable. When we finally arrived in Estella we just went into the municipal albergue which was very adequate at 6 euros per night. A party of Irish women teachers arrived in the late afternoon whose open, free and easy ways ensured there was "good craic". At night we went to the church of San Juan for Mass after which we, accompanied by Amelie, enjoyed a delicious meal of paella and duck. I had paella and Joe had duck. Amélie has a sunshiney nature, her eyes lighting up as she enthusiastically tells us of her family and life at home. She is well travelled and clearly made of strong stuff and I wonder how I might introduce her to my son Martin. We had to be in the albergue by 2200 with lights out by 2215!

Monday 25th March 2013

I slept very well and woke around 0600. As always when I wake at this time I lie and pray for my family commencing with the youngest grandchild and finishing with my wife. Then I start to pray for the wider family and friends and the world by which time it is either time to get up or I fall asleep again!

We rose at 0700 and were away by 0820 after coffee and a croissant on the way. Today the walk seemed easier at first and I met a chap we will call Bart. He is Californian, stands over six feet four inches and walks with a slight limp favouring his left leg. This is caused in part by some health issues including leukaemia and I feel sorry for him and admire his courage and tenacity. He is a fellow Christian and a really nice guy. We are able to talk for long periods of our shared experience of the goodness of God in Christ, then lapse into comfortable silences or walk apart till we close up again. For all he has a limp he can cover the ground quickly with his long strides.

The scenery and villages are beautiful, the architecture so old it looks Roman. We soon pass the Bodegas Irache where pilgrims may slake their thirst with the delicious wine which is on tap and free! From here we press on to Azqueta to view the 13th Century

*Cirauqui – The first picture I painted
from my Camino – 24th March*

Olive groves on the way from Cirauqui to Estella – 24th March

Fuente de Irache – Free wine from Bodegas Irache – 25th March

Montjardin to Los Arcos – 25th March

The Pension called Mavi in Los Arcos – 25th March

Fountain of the Moors, then make for Villamayor de Monjardin, nestling beneath its conical hill which is visible from some way off. We make our destination Los Arcos which is sleepy and very quaint, in the late afternoon, having clocked up 22 kilometres on arrival.

After finding a small *pensión* called Mavi we showered and went for some tapas called *pinchos* in this region. They filled a hole then we searched for and found a chemist which was the best I have ever seen for foot problems. Joe got some insoles and I some magic cream which actually worked to take the pain from the feet! I tried it on my shoulders and it worked there too! We will look for a *zapatería* to see if we can find Joe some lighter boots and me some dubbin - *betún de zapatos*. We had a nice meal in a restaurant also called Mavi owned by the people who owned our *pensión*, then got back by 2130 to turn in. It rained very heavily and did not bode well for the morrow.

Tuesday 26th March 2013

We woke at 0600 after a wonderful night's sleep and started getting ready from 0630. Even so it was 0812 before we left. I am putting these late departures down to Joe whose morning ablutions are epic in their complexity and thoroughness. I on the other hand settle for a couple of handfuls of cold water across the face. We were expecting rain but I think most had fallen overnight and we were in between the frontal systems. Not a drop – almost! As always our trail was picturesque and pleasant with a fair bit of hill climbing and descent. The stones cause the most pain which is deep inside – not surface blisters. I begin to understand the term "bone weary". Shoulders also get sore but otherwise no problems. Our path takes us through Sansol (I did not like it so much) then up the side of the 570 metre peak Nuestra Señora del Royo past the interesting ruins of Cornava. These are comprised of little beehive huts dotted here and there which would remind one of the cleits of St. Kilda. At last the road led downhill to the outskirts of Viana. We were accosted by a con-man who said he had been robbed and would have to retrace his steps on the Way. He was clearly a liar and stank of stale wine, but Joe gave him a euro anyway. It is a stiff climb through the suburbs of Viana, which are not attractive, but the old part is still beautiful and feels old. We took a room in the Casa Armendariz, which was most acceptable then delved into a big lunch of risotto and lamb stew, both of which were very tasty. At four o'clock everything stopped and everyone disappeared as usual. This takes a bit of getting used to, and we pilgrims from northern countries frequently discuss how foreign it is to our nature. I suspect that were we making the journey in summer we would begin to understand.

It rains and Joe and I lie weary on our beds. At 1800 we decide to move out and see the camping shop which should be open after siesta. It is shut and it is still raining. Heavily! We migrate, from doorway to doorway back to the church Iglesia de Santa María. We see big Bart in the forecourt of the church and go in. It is quiet but the lights are on and someone moves up to the lectern and begins the Rosary in Spanish. There is only one voice responding and I wish I could help but it is all "Ave Maria" and I am doctrinally inhibited. The great high altar is an extravaganza of Baroque theatre in praise of Santa María. We sit respectfully, contemplating the vastness of the church. It is a glorious celebration of Romano Gothic. After the Rosary the priest appears and begins the introduction for confessions. Once confessions start we can move around and view the rest of the church. It is overwhelmingly theatrical, each *capilla* containing some topic of

The hills to the north – 26th March

A square in Viana – 26th March

Inside Santa Maria in Viana – 26th March

The bridge into Logroño – 27th March

Logrono Cathedral – 27th March

The float bearing the statue of The Virgin leaving the cathedral – 27th March

The drum corps accompanying the statue of The Virgin – 27th March

Christ meeting his Mother – Logroño – 27th March

their belief system. By 2000 we have had enough and go down to a café which Bart has found. We order *pinchos* and a bottle of wine and say "Good evening" to Shane from Australia and his partner Emer from Eire, and little Estelle, to whom I spoke earlier on the trail. It is very jolly and friendly. About nine o'clock we break up and go to our separate lodgings. Joe and I are tired and are looking forward to sleep as we stretch out on our comfy beds.

Then the brass band strikes up directly across the narrow street on the same level as us, practising for *Semana Santa*. It is completely surreal! So we settle down to watch France playing Spain on the telly hoping that the practice is not too rigorous for the bandsmen and that we find a quieter billet tomorrow.

Wednesday 27th March 2013

We set off at the back of eight o'clock and journeyed through a landscape both rural and post- industrial. We are more used to walking now and our pace is steady. By 1100 we arrive into Logroño, where we will stop after a short day. We book into a hostel which is very plush. "Hostel Entresueños". The accommodation is pleasing to the eye and the facilities are good, so we shower and wash our clothes. In the afternoon we walk around with Bart who travelled from Viana with us. I like Bart very much. He is a conservative evangelical like me with a broad mind and kindly attitude; it is a real pleasure to walk with him. We trudge around the town all day and observe in passing that the preparations being made by the people of the cathedral and the great church of Santiago for *Semana Santa* are most exact and lovingly executed. They bring flowers and work hard to assemble the floats which will bear the effigy of the *Virgen* and a diorama of Christ bearing His cross.

Such a beautiful city - we take photographs all the time.

We find a camping equipment shop and Bart buys a jacket for the bad weather which currently assails us, and a walking pole, for his left leg is swelling up. I replace a lost towel. As evening approaches, I find an Aladdin's cave of a hardware store and manage to replace the steel tip of my stick, *punta del bastón*. The shopkeeper, when I describe my requirement, stands back for a moment behind his counter, shuts his eyes, as in prayer, then pounces on an unsuspecting drawer which holds exactly what I need. I am astonished that they can produce this, and then I realise that they have many implements which we no longer use in our post-agricultural country, and I see that it is we who are losing our roots in our past and with the land.

The rain comes on at around 1930 but the people are in the mood for *Semana Santa* and will the clouds away from the black sky.

The procession was quite overwhelming in its excitement and power. Many of the town of Logroño turned out to see. From the two churches – the Cathedral and from Iglesia Santiago – two distinct parties set out. In the procession from Santa María (the Cathedral) a statue of the Virgin, on an enormous ornate float is carried on the shoulders of about 28 men like the one in Pamplona. The statue is lit with electric lights powered by car batteries. Preceding the float, are a large company of attendants in tall hats and masks which cover the face, all wearing silk surcoats. There are different colours for different orders of devotees. This is quite intimidating enough, but it is the drummers, with a corps of about 40 drums of differing pitch which produce a terrific tattoo and set the pulse racing.

In the meantime, the same thing is happening at Iglesia Santiago. This procession bears a crucifixion diorama of Christ carrying His cross on a similar float, again with an attendant throng of hooded helpers, porters and drummers, now supplemented by a brass band. I wonder if it is the band of last night. Slowly the two groups process until they converge at a crossroads where there is a symbolic meeting of Christ and His Mother. At one point the two gigantic litters perform a brief nodding "dance". Then they make their way, accompanied by half the town to their respective churches. It is an unforgettable event. We get back to our lodgings at midnight!

Thursday 28th March 2013

We got away at the back of 8 o'clock accompanied by Bart. After coffee and croissants in a small *taberna* we were well on the trail by 0830. The going was good and we made good time in dry conditions, passing through Navarette where we had lunch. I had a fillet of chicken fried in beaten egg – delicious! With this, accompanied by coffee, bread and water, we were on the way again with a spring in our step. Around 1400 we arrived at Ventosa and went into a delightful albergue called San Saturnino. It has a lovely quiet ambience and it is run by an Austrian lady of middle years who has done the Camino many times. She has created a place of peace. She is assisted in this work temporarily by a beautiful young Hungarian woman and her husband whose names escape me. She is gentle and willing to listen. I speak to her about my love for Christ, but like so many she does not see His uniqueness, and would have all faiths in one. After lunch in the little bar near the albergue we walk around in sunshine and view the village.

In the evening we went to Mass and Joe and Bart took communion. I did not of course. I never have. Bart explains he was reared as a Catholic and only became an evangelical later in life. Somehow on Camino these fine divisions evaporate, and I think we begin to wear new spectacles which readjust our fixed perspectives. After Mass we processed around the village with the Crucifix and statue of Mary borne on the backs of the male parishioners. When we returned to the albergue we enjoyed an amicable time in the lounge with our fellow pilgrims accompanied by a bottle of red wine and wedge of goat's cheese. The fellowship was mellow and interesting. We had to have lights out by 2215.

Friday 29th March 2013

We were awakened at 0600 by the distant, measured mellifluence of Gregorian chant. It gently wooed us from slumber and persuaded us to rise and meet the day. After a simple breakfast of an orange and porridge, and a hug which I alone received from the beautiful young Hungarian woman who had clearly taken pity on the old man who spoke about his love for Christ, we were away by 7 o'clock to pass through Nájera and Azofra arriving at Cirueña around 1400. It was a hard day and the distance was more than the book says, for both by time and the pedometer it was about 26 kilometres. The rain came on around 1 o'clock in the afternoon and the last hour was very tough.

The lodgings we have found are very basic and called "Virgen de Guadeloupe". It is managed by a large man called Pedro who signs his art work which hangs in several places round the walls as "Petrus". Petrus has another worldly, distant cast to his eye. He thinks slowly and is imperturbable. Tonight he entertains not only we three men but also a gaggle of five Irish lady primary school

Breakfast Leaving Logroño – 28th March

The road to Navarette – 28th March

The old pilgrim route through Navarette – 28th March

Church of San Saturnino – Ventosa – 28th March

Holy Thursday procession , Ventosa -28th March

The path from Ventosa through Rioja vineyards – 29th march

Beehive hut built for pilgrims outside Nájera – 29th March

Nájera – Arabic for the Place Between The Rocks – 29th March

Our bunks in the Albergue Virgen de Guadeloupe, Ciruena – 29th March

Rioja landscape near Nájera – 29th March

*View from
the window –
Cirueña –
29th March*

*Happy pilgrims –
The Irish
school teachers –
Ciruena – 29th
March*

*Iglesia de San Andres
en Cirueña – 29th
March*

teachers. They are full of life and humour and merry banter passes easily round the table. Petrus has provided us with a simple meal based on lentils and vegetables. It is wholesome and filling and we are all thankful. We look forward to more luxury tomorrow.

After our meal we went to church. It was not well attended and the roof leaked in one corner over the aisle, and yet for me, in this simple quiet place with the rain beating down and in, I felt peace in my soul. We return and turn in around 2100. Our room, which we share with Bart, is cold and I persuade Petrus, in my pidgin Spanish, to provide a heater. This takes the form of an electric "flying saucer" shaped device which sits on the floor. We view it with suspicion, but within half an hour the temperature is markedly warmer. As we lie in our sleeping bags the wind freshens to a near gale and the shutters rattle against the old walls of our dwelling. I lie warm and cosy and remember nights on the North Atlantic when I was far from comfy and fall into a deep, deep, sleep feeling safe and well.

Saturday 30th March 2013

After a breakfast of toast and tea we got away from the albergue around 0800. We met up with the Irish teachers from Cork, Dublin and Galway who were such fun. The Camino soon separates us as we walk at different rates. One of the girls had very sore feet.

We felt good on the road and having made good time to Santo Domingo, decided to press on to Grañon. The albergue here is actually part of the church having once served as accommodation for monks and a refuge for pilgrims. The ambience is ancient and we access it by a very narrow spiral staircase let into the wall of the structure. This gives way to the first level sleeping area, currently just a large space with sanded floorboards, bare stone walls and paillasses stacked against the walls. It is however warm thanks, to modern central heating. We climb through another small door and staircase and arrive at the main hall where we are greeted by the *hospitalero.* He is an amiable young man who explains that we should fill in our details in the visitors' book. I am keen to obtain a stamp (*sello*) to record my visit, but strangely, the albergue does not possess one. This is truly extraordinary for these stamps are to be found everywhere so that pilgrims can prove they have visited a place. He offers instead a hug which we settle for. We are shown upstairs to a mezzanine floor overlooking the main eating hall. Here we can have a place on a mat on the wooden floor and sleep adjacent to complete strangers. The roof is exposed ancient timber beams which run down from its peak to a low stone wall on which we can place bits of gear.

After a hot shower I am better able to appreciate the feel of the place. It is old and worn and filled with interesting people. In the corner of the eating hall there is a wood burning stove around which people are draped on comfy chairs. One or two are playing instruments quietly and I allow my imagination to see characters from long ago. We have not changed so much, I muse; only the accidents change, the clothing, the hair, the speech. I could be looking at a diorama of five hundred years ago. They come on the Camino, each one with their own reasons. Some are looking for meaning and purpose. Some are working out problems and trying to make life decisions. That is not why I am here. My life is settled and has been lived to the full. I know my Saviour; I do not suffer from agnosis. I am able to come to God all day every day in Christ. I am here to expand my mind and my experience. To enjoy a significant event before I am no longer able, and I want to walk across Spain.

The Cathedral of Santo Domingo de Calzada – 30th March

Grañon – Church of San Juan Baptista – 30th March

Pilgrim accommodation – Grañon – 30th March

Flaked out under the ancient eaves- Grañon – 30th march

Pilgrim meal in the San Juan Baptista Albergue – Grañon – 30th March

Just before Easter Vigil Mass – Grañon – 30th March

The priest brings in the Light of Christ – Grañon – 30th March

For a donation the *hospitalero* and helpers produce a lovely meal which is enjoyed by all the pilgrims, sitting along the side of large trestle tables formed into a rectangle which occupies virtually the whole floor area. Before we begin to eat he asks if anyone would care to say grace. I leap at the chance for I am becoming concerned that I do not hear much about Christ on a Christian pilgrimage, and conclude my prayer "In Jesus' name, Amen".

After the meal Joe, Bart and I, along with some other pilgrims attend the adjoining church. It is connected to the albergue by a stone staircase of huge antiquity. The light in the church is subdued and there is a peace pervading the space. I realise that this Eastertide has been the most meaningful I have ever experienced.

This Easter Mass was not well attended. I suppose the congregation would not have numbered more than 60 souls. To be honest there was not much to differentiate it from a normal Sunday Mass, save when the lights were extinguished and the priest brought the Pascal candle into the dark church enabling us to light our candles from it. My son Joe takes a photograph which looks like a painting by Caravaggio. In the ancient darkness we symbolically spread the light of Christ amongst ourselves then celebrate the resurrection of the Lord. I am sad because the whole town and all the pilgrims are not in the church with us, and the thought occurs to me that I never saw a people more in need of the Gospel!

Sunday 31st March 2013

We rose about 0630 and made ready for the road. These preparations are made in half-light provided by various headlamps and torches. Everyone is afraid to flash a strong light in someone's direction and nobody wants to be the one to switch on the main light in case late sleepers are disturbed. Bart is one of the late risers as he has had a disturbed night, but eventually he succumbs to the muffled movement all round him and drags his not inconsiderable frame to the upright.

We breakfasted on left-over fruit salad from last night and toast, then set off for the longest walk of the trip so far. Our way led us through Redecilla de Camino, Castildelgado, Viloria de la Rioja, Villamayor del Rio, Belorado, Tosantos, Villambistia, Espinosa Del Camino, finally bringing us to Villafranca Montes de Oca. These villages and little towns are all delightful in their own way and many have existed as long as the Camino, because they exist for it. Passing through them demands that we photograph them because they are so full of interest and quaintness, and one is at a loss to make a choice of which particular topic to record.

This day we walked almost 29 kilometres. The last three were alleviated by the company of two Irish girls, who accompanied us. They had been at the albergue in Cirueña, utterly different to the one we now approached called San Anton Abad. It is truly beautiful and the room which Joe and I share has a shower with multi spray heads. This is unparalleled luxury and we each have difficulty turning the valve to shut when it comes to the end of our turn. After this therapy we repair to the conservatory-style bar for a beer and meet up with the two Irish girls. They have brushed up beautifully, and not for the first time I wonder at the female ability to achieve this transformation. It turns out that one of them is suffering from very painful blisters, but nothing can curtail their sense of fun. They relate how a truly kind German fellow had spent a long time fixing her feet on the trail and somehow it is what we have come to expect. Selfless kindness; in the true spirit

*Castildelgado, once a Roman town – the Church
of San Pedro – 31ˢᵗ March*

The Hermitage of Nuestra Señora de la Pena – 31ˢᵗ March

The Hotel San Anton Abad – 31st March

Hotel San Anton Abad – Villa Franca – 31st March

A well earned drink in the Hotel San Anton Abad – 31st March

Climbing to Alto Mojapan – 1st April

Coffee in San Juan de Ortega – 1st April

Our lovely hosts – Pilar and Miguel at Fortaleza – Orbaneja – 1st April

of pilgrimage. Conversation, as always, reveals that they are both, in their own way, very serious minded and are searching for answers to some of life's most challenging questions. The weather this day was halcyon but we knew when we lay down that night that we had worked hard.

Monday 1st April 2013

Six forty five is a good time to rise after a good night's rest, and having breakfasted on toast, yogurt and coffee in the same restaurant where we had dined the previous night, we were on the trail for 0810. We immediately started climbing the mountain Alto Mojapan (1100 metres). The path was steep, wet and stony but we kept the pace very slow and made steady progress. The way remained high and took in Alto Pedraja (1100 metres) and Alto Carnero (1150 metres). The terrain was fairly heavily forested with small oaks and firs of about 40 feet. It blew hard from the West North West all day but the rain stayed off and it was an exhilarating walk. The descent into San Juan de Ortega was initially quite steep but levelled out near the village. We dropped into a café only to meet the Irish girls from the night before. They must have made exceptionally good time. Their intention was to stop at Atapuerca the next village after Ages where we now were. Ages (pronounced Aches, with the *ch* as in loch) is well named for the houses are very ancient, many being timber framed in the Tudor manner. We decided to push on and climbed Alto Cruciero (1080 metres). The route took us into wilder country than we had seen so far and we felt very at home in the windy wilderness. We dropped down from the heights via a seldom used path to pass through Cardeñuela and on to Orbaneja where I was able to arrange a *casa rural*. This turned out to be a beautifully built holiday home and the couple who owned it, Pilar and Miguel, said they would cook us a meal that night.

The meal was delicious, consisting of garlic soup (with bread sops and onions), fried pork fillets, salad and salted tomatoes. This was followed by home-made café crème flavoured with orange. After dinner we sampled Miguel's delicious home-made wine and Joe, Bart, Miguel, Pilar and I all sat and conversed freely. I was even persuaded to play the chanter briefly. We turned in around 10 o'clock and slept soundly.

Tuesday 2nd April 2013

It was a cold, misty morning with a slight drizzle falling, when we woke around 0700 and made ready to go by 0800. We breakfasted in the nearest café and set off for Burgos. The path was quiet but led us through industrial areas until we reached the river when it became greener and therefore more picturesque. The river was very full and flooding in places. We arrived at the Hotel Norte Y Londres around noon and obtained a beautiful room. Joe and I went for a fantastic meal which Joe, who is generosity itself, reckoned we needed. He has been overwhelmingly kind to me on this trip and inside I know that when he leaves, as he will from Burgos, I will miss him immensely. After the meal we went to the cathedral which was architecturally and visually staggering - and very cold! It is truly beautiful. As we completed our tour Bart contacted us to say that he had met up with the two Irish girls in a hostelry and invited us to join them. We did and there followed several hours of socialising for there was a carnival atmosphere in the air as the girls were going home on the morrow, and so was Joe. Enough said.

The mighty steeples of Burgos Cathedral – 2nd April

The Altar – Burgos Cathedral – 2nd April

Cloisters – Burgos Cathedral – 2nd April

The Meseta – Time for introspection – 3rd April

Hornillos – 3rd April

Albergue at Hornillos – good fellowship – 3rd April

Wednesday 3ʳᵈ April 2013

We woke to the alarm at 0600 and Joe was his usual self – plus a headache! I gave him a couple of painkillers and he rallied quickly. He is very fit. He was soon ready and I saw him off at 7 o'clock in a taxi. He caught his train fine and I was alone. To be quite candid this is my favourite condition. I have spent a great deal of my life with my own company having been in command at sea for so long, so while I was sorry to see my son depart, at the same time the road ahead beckoned with further encounters and experiences. I therefore set off with a light heart after breakfast and soon met up with an English chap whom I am calling Denis. He was two years younger than I and we plodded along at an old man's pace. It was very comfortable. Leaving via the west gate we made steady progress through Villabilla, Tardajos, and Rabe de Las Calzados, then climbed steadily up and onto the Meseta. It is beautiful rolling countryside with what appears to be very limey soil which does not look promising but seems to be very fertile. The skies are big and the horizon stretches away forever like the sea, inducing the same introspection and contemplative frame of mind. Of course the small *pueblos* mentioned above are very beautiful and I took several photos. Sometimes my interest was captured by a tiny window let into an ancient wall; sometimes by a door which appeared to have been hung in the Middle Ages. When we arrived at the albergue at Hornillos Del Camino, we discovered the *casa rural* which my companion had booked into was flooded! So he elected to accept a run to the next village to find another *casa rural*. I think he was not impressed by the albergue in which I and most of the pilgrims intended to spend the night. I was sorry because he was a fine chap. The rest of us hung around for a while but there was no sign of the *hospitalera*. We heard from a local worthy that she was in the bar. This sounds much worse than it was for after some time I went over to the bar to find her. She was not, as some of us speculated, imbibing. She was just having a well- deserved coffee. She immediately came over after about five minutes, which is immediate in Spain, and those of us who were hanging around were signed in. When I had selected my bunk I had a wonderful shower and freshened up. Along with some nice Alaskan young folk comprising a married couple, Abel and Lydia, and the girl's brother, Amos, all hailing from Kodiak Island, and a couple of New Zealand ladies, Melissa and Charlotte, we made our way back to the bar to eat. It was closed. This necessitated returning at 5 o'clock and, choosing from the daily pilgrim's menu, were able to fill ourselves and be well satisfied. The pilgrim's menu I find is unswerving in its uniformity on the Camino, with only minor variations from place to place. As long as they had hake and *flan*, which is actually crème caramel, I was quite happy. After dinner the rain came on heavily and we had to run back to the albergue. By now the lady in charge, whom we had inwardly calumniated, was making up the fire in the pilgrims' communal lounge and things really started to look up. Quite a few of us from at least five nationalities sat round the table, near the fire and conversed in a mixture of our several languages. It was great fun. One of the New Zealand ladies, when I told her my shoulder was sore, offered to massage it for me. She had this cream which had been specially prepared in New Zealand by a Maori medicine man, and I was glad to have someone who cared enough to do something about my pain. Sure enough she set to work, with me stripped to the waist in front of the other pilgrims, and I can say without a shadow of doubt that it helped immensely. It was a lovely act of kindness. When I turned in I fell into a deep sleep, lying almost as close to the New Zealand lady as I would to my own wife, so close were the bunks and so full was the albergue.

Thursday 4th April 2013

I rose while it was still dark and set out with the advancing dawn, after an orange and a cup of hot chocolate! This is not my normal breakfast by any stretch of the imagination, but the Camino is an opportunity for firsts. We pilgrims are adaptable! On leaving the albergue the light was growing as I made my way alone over the Meseta towards the first staging post, the hamlet of San Bol. I revelled in the lonely road and as far as I was concerned there was no one else on the Camino. After about ten kilometres I arrived at Hontanos where I had coffee. I met up with a German I had first come across in Grañón. He had already been in the bar about three quarters of an hour and was moving on which pleased me, for I was able to complete the walk via San Anton to Castrojeriz alone. This is how I like to walk. On arrival it was raining heavily but I met an old man leaving his home with his wet weather gear on, and when I had asked for directions, he insisted on accompanying me and leading me to a camping gear store which looked and felt like a trading post of yesteryear. I bought a poncho to shun the heavy rain, some dubbin and a new clip for the waist belt of my rucksack. The original had failed and without it my shoulder ached abominably. I then signed into the albergue which lay close alongside the camping store. It was spacious and pleasant with more room between the tiers of bunks, which was just as well for I would spend that night as well adjacent to an American lady who was a writer/reporter with the Wall Street Journal. After the arriving pilgrims had showered, we met up for a meal in the restaurant El Cordon after a glass of wine in the bar called El Mesón. The meal was typical pilgrim menu but it sufficed. I said grace and we enjoyed fellowship. We were back in the hostel by 2130 and all in bed by 10 P.M. we all just wanted to sleep but not before my half Maori masseuse had given me a "proper" massage in the open space of the dormitory for half an hour in front of all the other pilgrims. This was a source of great mirth and *sotto voce* ribaldry, but I was so grateful for I was in considerable pain. The Wall Street journalist who slept in the tier of bunks adjacent to me was a fascinating woman, who, having been widowed with two children, now adults, had set up a gay partnership with a woman older than her.

Friday 5th April 2013

The hostel began to waken around 0615 and we all groped around as usual, all averting our gaze in the near-darkness for the sake of preserving some semblance of privacy. After a quick breakfast – I had porridge from home and tea, the pilgrims set off in fits and starts on the Camino. Rachael the American journalist and I walked together for a while then I went on ahead at my own pace, reaching Itero de la Vega around 1030. It had been a good pull over the Alto Mostelares so I stopped for coffee in a bar. As I sat there relishing the taste of the coffee which in Spain even when decaffeinated never seems to disappoint, I saw the Wall Street journalist heave into view. When we left the bar we went on together.

Rachael makes an excellent travelling companion as she is intelligent and well read. She also has co-authored a book about the period leading up to the collapse of Enron. The next village was Boadilla Del Camino which we walked straight through, preferring to snack briefly amid a pile of hay bales on the outskirts of the village. I am fairly sure it is the same heap of bales they used to shoot a certain scene in the film "The Way". From there it was 6 short kilometres to Frómista where we dined, then booked into a hotel called San Martín, which was most appropriate as this

The owner and my Good Samaritan inside the pilgrim trading post Castrojeriz – 4th April

Approaching Castrojeriz – 4th April

*My fellow pilgrim friends at dinner in El Cordon
Restaurant – Castrojeriz – 4th April*

*Early morning view of Castrojeriz from Alto
Montelores – 5th April*

The lock at the end of the Canal de Castilla - Fromista – 5th April

The 11th Century Church of St. Martin of Tours
– Frómista – 5th April

Población de Campos – 6th April

8 PM service in Santa Maria la Blanca – Carrion de los Condes – 6th April

day is my son Martin's birthday. My room is luxurious and I revel in the unashamed decadence of soaking in a bath without constantly looking out for others. I followed this by doing my washing and phoning Patsy. It was good to speak to her and hear her report of our family. Patsy is a communicator extraordinaire. She would have made a superb interrogator for Military Intelligence, for she misses nothing. I went out around half past six and bought some insoles for my sandals and some arnica-based cream for all purposes. This cream is made by the chemist himself so I hope that it comes with the experience of millennia, which he assures me it does.

I went to church at 8 PM. It was a Mass which was being celebrated on the feast of St.Elmo. It was attended by large numbers of loud young folk in their twenties and thirties, dressed in a sort of uniform comprising bib and brace trousers and a jupon or battledress jacket with the logo PEÑA across the back. These uniforms appear to be brightly coloured according to whichever club or association one belongs. After communion most of the young men repaired to the choir balcony and there began to sing with great gusto and enthusiasm a hymn in praise of St.Elmo. I had a feeling that some were filled with a spirit other than that of the Lord, but at least they wanted to participate. After the dismissal they all, accompanied by similarly dressed wives, sweethearts and children, repaired to the bar of my hotel! I feared my early night of peaceful reflection and well-earned slumber was evaporating before my eyes, although as it turned out my misgivings were unfounded for I slept very soundly till seven in the morning.

Saturday 6th April 2013

I set off before it was fully light and was soon hailed by a young woman (*¡hola peregrino!*) who informed me I had missed the road. She was dressed in the uniform of the night before and had been up all night partying as part of the association called PEÑA. I thanked her for alerting me to my mistake and asked her what PEÑA was. She told me in good English that it was an association of clubs of young people who lived to drink and have a good time! She told me that the youth of Spain were utterly disillusioned with almost every facet of life and that the recession was bearing down heavily upon them so much so they wanted to escape each weekend into bacchanalian frolics. She said that most of the young folk were in commerce of some sort or another. I replied that this morning she had been kind enough to put me on my right road and I now I wished to tell her that I truly believed that she and her friends were on the wrong road of life and that there was another Way. I told her of my love for Christ and the wonderful life He had given me when He saved me from going down the road she was now on. Two fine strapping young fellows, who had also been up all night were listening to what I was saying and I had the impression the Holy Spirit was at work there in the half-light of dawn, on the long flat road leading out of Frómista.

This is not a very interesting part of the Camino which passes by low-lying flat lands and through Población de Campos, Villacazar de Sirga to Carrión de los Condes. I arrived there just after noon, well ahead of everyone, and chose to stay in the Monasterio de Santa Clara for I understood St. Francis of Assisi had stayed there on his pilgrimage so long ago. I feel an affinity to St. Francis as that is the name of our pipe band. The *hospitalero* stamped my *credencial* then took me on a rapid, well-rehearsed tour of the accommodation and facilities. It was pleasant and clean and was looked after immaculately by the nuns who were cloistered there. I was the only pilgrim in the place, and then little by little it began to fill up with many folk I had travelled with before. I went out for lunch, bought a charger which could charge anything I was likely to want to charge, and met Jacinta and François, who I had bumped into several times during the pilgrimage. Every time I speak to Jacinta she speaks to me in fluent Spanish which strangely, I seem to get the gist of, I think more by body language than anything else. François is frequently in her vicinity and I think they are simpatico. Jacinta is very Spanish, lean and wise, her hair pulled back in a tight bun. François is very French and quiet and provincial and comfy. They are friendly and companionable to each other and everyone else. Around five o'clock, Rachael, Melissa, Charlotte (also from New Zealand and the friend of Melissa) and the young folk from Alaska appear. I am delighted to see them all and they are given the tour by the *hospitalero*. I am beginning to form the opinion that he is a "wee soul" given this work out of love and sympathy by the nuns. The Camino is amazing in the way it continually throws people together again and again.

It is cold in the monastery but I reckon once all the bodies heat up it will be fine. In the evening a bunch of us went out for an evening meal and enjoyed a lovely time of fellowship. I had soup, a fish course of hake which forms the bulk of my staple diet, and a glass of wine. We were all in bed by ten. On returning we found out that one of our fellow pilgrims, a South Korean chap, had had his money stolen in the albergue in Boadilla Del Camino. The thief, whoever he was, took all his cash and threw away his passport which was thankfully found by someone. We all felt pretty bad about this and Marco a young man of Italian descent residing in London piped up in a Cockney-Italian accent that maybe we should chip in to help him so we did and left it under his pillow. When he found it he was touched and it went some way to restore his faith in humanity. I do not know if he will be able to complete the Camino.

Sunday 7th April 2013

I got up after a good night's sleep and set off at 0730. It was just coming on light and I was walking with a good pace. I had the path more or less to myself and soon began overhauling people who had left really early. I passed quite a few then around ten o'clock came on a German chap called Karl. After the usual pleasantries and chit chat he asked me why I was doing the Camino and I gave him what is becoming my stock answer, namely that I am not here to find salvation for I have found it already in Jesus Christ. I am not resolving big problems for I do not have any, so I guess I am going for a walk, although as I go along I am forming the opinion that I have a ministry to declare the Gospel whenever it is required. This was the case with Karl and it seems some of the things I said helped him! I praise God for this, because it gives a purpose to what I am doing which I did not expect. It is the greatest joy to be told you have helped someone. Karl and I parted at Ledigos and I promised to pray for him. All day long we had been walking the Via Aquitania and I marvelled again at that amazing nation, the Romans, who turned Europe into a civilized place. I know they had huge faults but they are still worthy of admiration. At length I arrived at Terradillos de Templarios where I checked in to a beautiful new albergue called Los Templarios. It was well appointed and I could not resist the temptation of obtaining a room for 20 Euros – luxury! Clearly I am not embracing the self-denial aspect of pilgrimage as fully as I might although the *albergue* was cold, and I struggled for oblivion.

*Looking like Hobbit dwellings – Bodegas
for storing wine – 7th April*

Via Aquitania – Dead straight! – 7th April

Ruins of the 9th Century Monastery of San Facundo – 8th April

Sahagún built on the ruins of a Roman town – 8th April

17ᵗʰ Century San Benito Arch – Sahagún – 8ᵗʰ April

Calzada Romana the road to Calzadilla de los Hermanillos – 8th April

Mansilla de las Mulas – siesta time! – 9th April

Fellow pilgrims from Ireland in Mansilla de las Mulas – 9th April

I woke several times during the night, not with cold, but because of a dog which insisted in barking at its shadow. Every now and again "Bark-Bark! Pause... Bark-Bark! I hated that dog by morning! Ah yes, and I met up with the Englishman, Denis, whose company I enjoy. I tend to become disconnected from him for he walks at a different pace and seldom uses the albergues, preferring the *casas rurales*. I think one misses a great deal by avoiding the albergues altogether although I agree one needs privacy from time to time.

Monday 8th April 2013

I eventually gave up and got up around 0700. Even ear-plugs would not keep the dog out! I was on the road by 0745 and began the 26.9 kilometre hike towards Calzadilla de los Hermanillos. The way passes through Moratinos, San Nicolás del Real Camino, and Calzada de Coto. It was a long hard road and the wind blew strongly making it even longer and harder. The landscape is really very flat, relieved by olive groves and stands of pale barked trees, whose name I do not know. They are planted in serried ranks and have a mystical dimension to them. They are like silent observers of the passing pilgrims. I will paint these trees for they have been my companions for some time and they intrigue me. I am not often given to metaphysical thoughts about natural things but for some reason these trees make me think of sentinels. I arrived at the albergue Via Trajana in the early afternoon and took a room which I share with tall big-boned Irishman I have called Nial from Drogheda. I get on well with Irishmen and this fellow is no exception. We are berthed at the very top of the house in an attractively decorated room. The wind is howling outside and it is very cosy.

I woke at midnight with a pressing urge to use the facilities and so began a period of intense diarrhoea which assailed me relentlessly till morning and caused me to feel very tired.

Tuesday 9th April 2013

The frequent demands to use the facilities were very debilitating but my big Irish room-mate was travelling to Mansilla de las Mulas by taxi as his foot had a bad blister. So I asked him to take a load of my gear with him to lighten my pack. I am glad I did for our day covered 24.3 kilometres of flat agricultural land. It was a difficult time and I felt weak and weary and worried about disgracing myself all day, but I had another four Irishmen and Denis for company so it passed well enough with plenty of good banter and an opportunity now and then to talk about Christ. The trail lay across countryside which was flat but not uninteresting, for the vibrant colours in the clear air made it easy to pick out villages and little towns from a long way off. Eventually we arrived in Mansilla de los Mulas where big Nial had booked his four companions and me into a *pensión*

I am berthed with Cecil, a witty and intelligent fellow in his middle fifties from Dublin. He makes me think of a character from James Joyce and speaks with a cultured Dublin accent. We all walk around together after a siesta and go for a meal, but I can eat nothing. I buy some electrolyte in a pharmacy with which I hope to stabilise my gut. Tomorrow, on the advice of the guide-book, we decide to take a bus into León where Patsy has booked me into a very plush hotel for two nights as a prize for getting half-way. I need to recuperate and am pretty worn out. I have about 360 kilometres to go but it is over quite mountainous terrain and I will have to work the journey out carefully, trying to keep to 20 kilometres or less every day. That was the third long day on the trot and my shoulder aches even with the lighter pack. I turn in early, not feeling too bright.

My room-mate was supposed to return around 2300 but does not appear till half past midnight! Yes, he is very, very drunk and after waking me wants to help me. His heart is in the right place but all I want to do is to be left alone. He finally settles down after one in the morning muttering a wide selection of Irish and English oaths directed mostly, I think, at his fellow Irish travellers. As the night wears on I am wracked from time to time by my poor waste disposal system, and to compound my misery a nasty haemorrhoid has formed in a location most likely to cause pain and discomfort. Eventually exhaustion takes over and I drift into a nightmare-riven sleep.

Wednesday 10th April 2013

I woke at 0800 and started getting organised. Cecil was full of apologies and was suffering from alcohol-induced amnesia. I was afraid I would let myself down on the bus so decided to take a taxi. I arrived in León just after 0900 and my room was available for which I thanked God heartily. I arranged through the splendid hotel staff to see a doctor at a health centre some distance from the hotel and after a short wait was examined by the duty doctor. He declared there was nothing actually wrong with my gut but prescribed electrolytes to replace salts and put me on a diet of apple and yogurt for breakfast and fish or chicken with boiled potatoes and carrots for dinner. This suited me down to the ground. He checked my blood pressure which astounded me at 100/70. I could not believe it but there it is. It was easy to obtain my medicine which cost the princely sum of one euro and fifty

Lobby of Hotel San Isidoro – León – 10th April

My room in the San Isidoro – 10th April

The Cathedral de Santa Maria in León – built on the site of 2nd Cent. Roman baths – 11th April

Some of the many stained glass windows of León Cathedral - 11th April

cents in the pharmacy near the health centre. This was a most reassuring outcome so I made my way back to my beautiful hotel, where I crawled under a lovely warm blanket and slept for two hours! When I awoke I arranged for my washing to be done, had a haircut, booked an appointment to see a physiotherapist on the morrow, obtained a clasp for the waist-belt of my rucksack, designed and ordered 100 business cards for the promotion of my book, and visited the museum which was part of my hotel the San Isidoro. It was a busy day. On Patsy's insistence I will try to eat something in the restaurant tonight.

Thursday 11th April 2013

Considering I had napped during the afternoon and was up to my gunwales in electrolyte, occasioning the necessary nocturnal visits to the chamber of easement, I slept remarkably well. I rose about 0800 and took a light breakfast of toast, yogurt and weak tea. Outside the rain fell determinedly as I set out to find my physiotherapist. I had actually obtained the address of this surgery from a business card I happened to pick up in the albergue in Mansilla de los Mulas and thankfully the hotel staff were able to give me directions. I trudged around the streets of León in my electric blue poncho, making a couple of abortive circuits of the old city walls before I got my bearings, but eventually I arrived at the place with a few minutes to spare. I was put into the hands, literally, of a beautiful 22 year old girl called Licinia, which her friends had abbreviated to "Lithy". I told her that the shortening of her lovely Roman name was a great shame and advised her to insist on the full name but of course she would ignore that advice. Nevertheless we discussed many things for an hour, as I lay supine, face down gazing at the floor through an oval aperture. Under her skilful manipulations my shoulder is much improved. The rain continued to fall relentlessly as I left the surgery and made my way back to the hotel, to lunch on apple (*manzana*) and natural yogurt, and after a sinfully indulgent hot shower, slept for two hours. I am clearly very tired, and having committed the grave error of allowing a woman hairdresser to trim my beard, have assumed a hunted and haggard look. However I rose at 4 PM and sallied forth into the windy sunshine, for the frontal system which had brought the heavy rain had passed on to leave blustery, sunny showers.

León cathedral is stunning from every point of view, but for me as I wandered around it felt bereft of the Holy Spirit and had assumed the mantle of an overwhelmingly beautiful museum. When it was built it must have been able to hold thousands of worshippers but now, because of the successive building of subsidiary chapels and special areas which are fenced off from common use by mighty railings, I think it would be hard put to hold a congregation of more than a few hundred. I visited the gantry they have erected to carry out restoration and it gave a true impression of the work of the wonderful stone masons who built the place.

When I had had enough, for I was by now suffering from museum fatigue, I picked up my business cards which look very swish in a subdued and gentlemanly manner, and bought a spare pair of boot laces which I reckoned I would soon need. I intend to promote my book unashamedly.

There is a strange phenomenon in Spain which seems to be that the better the hotel, the later will be dinner. On my return to the hotel I hung around for dinner which would be cooked especially for me, and would comprise chicken and boiled potatoes and carrots. It was very tasty but my appetite was poor, so I repaired to my room and having watched television which was fixated on the floods in various parts of Spain, (I had first-hand knowledge of this), and the financial crisis with which I had complete sympathy having experienced similar cash flow problems myself in the past, I fell asleep to be roused at 4 AM for the usual reasons and noise coming from people returning from a night out to the next room. Thankfully they soon fell asleep and so did I.

Friday 12ᵗʰ April 2013

Because of my weakened condition and the pain in my shoulder I decided to reduce further the amount I carried each day by sending on by car about half the weight of equipment I normally carried , using a company called Jacotrans. For this service they charged me seven euros. Even so I was still carrying about eight kilogrammes, but this arrangement transformed my enjoyment of the walk, for the pain in my shoulder was markedly lessened. This would be my method of operation from now on until I reached Santiago. I found it very easy to decide how far I would travel and where I would be at night so it was just a question of choosing an albergue which I hoped would be suitable. This added a certain frisson to the trip for I had no idea what my night's accommodation would be like and I looked forward to the uncertainty of my lodgings. On almost every occasion the hostel would be entirely satisfactory.

In the morning, therefore, I quickly prepared my duffle bag for sending on to the albergue in Villar de Mazarife, whereupon I consumed a "hearty" breakfast of apple and yogurt in my room and having completed the packing of my rucksack took a taxi to Virgen Del Camino to avoid the outskirts of León. There I alighted, and began a tough walk over wild country in a gale of wind and rain which sought unsuccessfully to penetrate my waterproof defences. The trail passed through Fresno Del Camino, Oncina, and Chozas de Abajo. As I plodded along the windswept, rain-lashed path, I retreated into myself and existed in a little cocoon of warm discomfort, for my gut was still extremely disturbed; my piles were making themselves felt and my shoulder, although much improved by massage and a lighter pack, was still painful. As the morning turned into afternoon I began to yearn for somewhere to stop and prayed that the Lord would lead me to a place where I could be helped.

On reaching Villar de Mazarife I cast around for the albergue but did not at first find the place I had sent my extra gear on to. This occasioned much praying, for conditions were deteriorating and at length I found the place I was looking for. I was met by Pepe, an older man with a lined, sallow face, his chin and cheeks covered in greying stubble, his eyes, bright and intelligent, quickly assessing this new arrival to his threshold. He was accompanied by Nuria, a lovely, dark haired, young woman of around thirty years with kind eyes and a quiet, caring nature. As I sloughed off my sodden gear in the hallway and asked if there was a doctor nearby, she said "You have come to the right place. The man who owns this albergue (Pepe) is a doctor of natural medicine and has great knowledge; listen to him for he is a great healer". I was a little taken aback by this for the last thing I wanted was a "quack" doctor, but there was something so kind and caring about this pair that I decided to go along with it, for I sensed they knew what I needed. (I could almost hear my son Joe scorning this decision for he is first and foremost a man of science.) As far as I was concerned, for the first time in days I felt I was speaking to people who cared. Nuria, whose Arabic name means "Light of Heaven", asked me to sit down at the end of the large table which I would learn later was the dining table for all the pilgrims. In the meantime Pepe had retreated to the comfort of a chair beside a wood burning stove in the corner of the dining hall for a quick smoke. I was prepared to be unfazed by this as I had once been attended to by an ophthalmologist in Kawasaki who did a splendid job of removing a splinter of paint from my eyeball, and he smoked throughout the minor operation! Having finished his cigarette Pepe came over to my corner and sat down beside me. By this time Nuria had produced a small bottle of sweet almond oil, a little of which Pepe rubbed on his hands. He then proceeded to push the blood in the veins of my bared right forearm from my wrist up to my elbow, and felt for the return of the blood to the empty veins. He did this several times but did not find what he was looking for. He then got me to take off my watch and did the same thing with my left forearm. Suddenly he seemed to detect what he wanted, indicating the diagnostic marker by tapping a certain point on my forearm lightly. He prescribed Camomile tea with lemon juice, sugar and a little bicarbonate of soda. This concoction had an immediate soothing effect, and for the first time in days I began to feel improved. In the meantime, Nuria was preparing pumpkin soup and having set down a large steaming bowl invited me to eat. I wolfed it down like a starving man. She said "You will want to eat tonight for your appetite will return". Then out of the blue she said "You are not going to die, and you *will* finish the Camino". This was very comforting news on both counts and encouraged me to confess to the existence of my haemorrhoids. She disappeared and returned with a cone from a cypress tree which caused me to shuffle uncertainly in my seat, anticipating her next revelation. She instructed me to keep it in my right pocket! Note, my right pocket, no other pocket would do, nor was I to be concerned about taking my trousers off at night for the effect of the cone in the right pocket during the day was sufficient. I was prepared to try all things and resolved to keep the cone in my pocket until it sprouted! (When I returned home, my Google enquiries revealed not only that the cypress cone is a time-honoured cure for piles but also that the tea of the cypress cone will stop internal bleeding).

Shortly after my treatment, having taken a shower which further enhanced the returning sense of well- being, I fell into conversation with a lady from Watford, who also was having a job discerning why she had come on Camino, for it had been a brutal day. Her gentle nature and quiet conversation were most welcome to me, for she, having five children and four grandchildren was astonished to find someone who trumped her for offspring. We had many common experiences to share and the time to dinner passed very pleasantly.

That evening we pilgrims, for our company had now swollen to about twenty in number, enjoyed a lovely meal cooked by Nuria and Pepe, my own diet being carefully controlled by them. Pepe personally cooked me two pieces of hake and brought them to the table. I later asked Nuria about what my diet should be for the morrow and she said "You can eat anything, you are cured!" My surprise clearly showed for she said "Stop thinking about it." At this she pinched a morsel of air from beside her temple and with a dismissive gesture released it to the ether "Put it away just like that!"

That night I slept well, rising only once.

Saturday 13th April 2013

The day dawned with a thin fog covering the area with the promise of better weather to come and for the first time in a long time it looked as though we might get sunshine. I got away at the

The Passage of Honour (Paso Honroso) Jousting Tournament – 13th April

The pilgrim meal in the Albergue San Antonio de Padua – Villar de Mazarife – 12th April

Some of the paintings in Albergue San Miguel – 13th April

The bunks in Albergue San Miguel – 13th April

*Hospital de Órbigo –
13th April*

*My bed in
Pension Garcia
– 14th April*

Former Bishops Palace – Astorga – 14th April

back of 0800 and walked alone making good time with only one stop at Villavante for essential purposes and a cup of tea. I was in Hospital de Orbigo by 1200, having logged 14.3 kilometres. I could easily have carried on for I was feeling noticeably stronger but I wished to pace my recovery and in any case I would have missed this lovely old village which has so much history. Not for the first time it occurred to me that if one wanted to see what streets were like in ancient Rome one should come to Spain and walk the Camino.

The albergue I have come to is called San Miguel. It is warm and welcoming with a delightfully cosy feel to it. It appears to be a repository for the work of pilgrim artists inspired by the Camino, for the walls are everywhere hung with their work. Some of the pieces are excellent, exhibiting truly mature talent. The albergue is a refurbished, very old house and has all one could want for 8 euros a night including breakfast. I am writing this in the patio in a warm afternoon sun; I am clean and my health is rapidly improving. The *hospitalero* tells me the "Los Ángeles" is a good restaurant for fish so I will visit it tonight and sample their cuisine.

The restaurant was fine offering the usual pilgrim style meal commencing with *ensalada mixta*. I chose trout as my main dish and was not disappointed. I dined with several pilgrims who were by now becoming familiar to me, so our conversation, having long ago progressed beyond the banal, was both interesting and stimulating. I had met a lady from London in the afternoon, who represented for me an archetypal "high flyer", numbering Lever Brothers amongst her clients. She advised them about their corporate persona. In her forties, with clean cut, attractive, angular features, she was fit and lean and very driven for she was determined to walk at least thirty kilometres a day to meet her schedule. On hearing I had written a book she immediately ordered a copy by sending a text to her husband. That afternoon, before dinner, we sat in the sunshine on the pavement accompanied by a friendly young man of African extraction who had spent most of his life in Sweden and the United States. He spoke both Swedish and Texan English perfectly. Such are the diverse characters the pilgrim will rub shoulders with.

When we returned to the albergue there was a party in full swing in the patio I had sat in earlier. To be fair the party broke up at 2200 but the giggling and rustling, as the erstwhile revellers prepared for bed went on for another hour. I find this hard to cope with and eventually, in my North Atlantic sea captain's voice told them to go to sleep – which they did. My biggest problem on the Camino is the shared facilities and communal living, and yet I am bound to admit that some of my most interesting memories so far have come from life in the albergues.

Sunday 14th April 2013

Normality was restored to my personal plumbing system at 0400 and I am both much more comfortable and deeply grateful. I was up and about with the usual mêlée and breakfasted by 0800, whereupon I set off initially with a helpful English lady I have called Joyce, who was very knowledgeable about the various stopping places on the Way; she had done it once before and now spoke to women's meetings about the subject with some authority. Unfortunately we walked at very different rates and I soon left her behind only to catch up with an amiable Irishman, whom I shall call Diarmid. Before long we were joined by a lady from Finland called Lisa and we three had a splendid walk to Astorga via Santibáñez de Valdeglesia and San Justo de la Vega. I picked up my extra gear as arranged from the municipal albergue where the *hospitalero* had kindly agreed to look after it till I arrived. I simply could not bear another night of shared facilities so I thanked him profusely, offered to pay for his trouble, which he resolutely refused, and eventually found a *pensión* called "García".

The *pensión* is old, tired, jaded and populated by old men living out their last days! I sense another Hemingway location, for I have been mulling over Hemingway since Pamplona and discreetly examine the faces of my fellow lodgers, fascinatingly tanned, lined and worn by the climate of northern Spain, inviting speculation about their lives. Had they been active in the civil war? Had they reared families who now had no time for them? Were there any unsung heroes among them? It was disturbing to imagine myself in a similar scenario in the future and I resolved to stay friends with my children.

After a shower in the diminutive bath, which was about a metre long, and mastering the aging plumbing, I felt good and slept for an hour. I dreamt about re-securing showerheads to walls all over Spain for even in the best hotels I invariably find them either loose or off the wall completely!

I kept to myself that evening not out of choice, but just because that's the way it worked out. Eventually around seven thirty I found a plush looking restaurant which was serving food from eight o'clock. I was shown to a table in a corner which gave me an ideal position to survey my fellow diners and allowed myself to be persuaded to try the steak on the recommendation of the waiter. The photograph on the menu looked truly gigantic to my meat starved eyes and I reasoned that in view of my recent enforced ascetic diet my body needed the protein and so justified the 22 euros which it cost. It was truly delicious, and the steak, helped on its way by sips of the house Rioja wine created a glow of well-being and contentment, allowing me to discreetly study the couples around me.

It is fascinating to watch other folk as you eat your dinner, to study the nuances of body language and the subtle implication of a gesture or glance. I am able to deduce (probably entirely erroneously) the status of the several couples, whether they are happy to be together, tolerating each other or downright fed up with each other. I notice one fellow in particular who is clearly trying to impress the woman he is with but enjoys indifferent success. He is trying too hard and coming across as a "wide boy" or a corrupt car salesman. He has my sympathies for she is an attractive woman.

I spy another couple well down the road of life. They look as though they are discussing grandchildren, that joyously interminable topic for older couples who have long since left off trying to impress each other. The grandmother has much to say and the grandfather has no option but to listen and agree. It's what one does for a quiet life. His mind is probably thinking about planting beans in the allotment in the very near future, as the ground is heating up and spring is in the air.

There is a German couple some forty feet away, having an altercation with the waiter who is calmly rebutting the aggression of his client, the former adamant that he ordered certain tapas which have not appeared. Eventually the irate German calls for assistance from another German-speaking couple (I think they are Swiss) to translate for him and little by little an international incident is avoided and resolved. The Teutonic male ego is partially satisfied by this intercession and the healing process is completed by the gentle stroking by his partner's hand, because that is what wise women do.

Monday 15th April 2013

I spent a comfy night in the Pensión García but had to transfer my gear back to the municipal albergue for uplift by Jacotrans as the owners did not work with Jacotrans. Again the *hospitalero* of Siervas de María was kindness and understanding itself, refusing any consideration, and he assured me he would see that it was uplifted and sent on. I finally cleared away from Astorga by 0900 and soon started overtaking people. The steak was working! I walked most of the day alone passing through Murias de Rechivaldo, Santa Catalina, and Ganso arriving at Rabanal around 1330. The albergue I wanted to stay in, which is owned and run by the Confraternity of St. James, of which I am a member, was shut for another hour, so I left my gear on their doorstep and found the other albergue called Nuestra Señora de Pilar where my extra equipment had been delivered. They were open all day and had no qualms about taking in gear from Jacotrans so I decided to patronise them for their kindness and treated myself to the ubiquitous *ensalada mixta* and a can of Aquarius. This is a still water drink containing some electrolytes and flavouring which quenches the thirst and replaces some salts.

The albergue Gaucelmo was worth waiting for as it is well organised, scrupulously clean and tranquil. They have a regime which I liked for it seemed to have been set up with the idea of Christian pilgrimage at the heart of the existence of the place. I for one could have asked for no more, because after I had showered, done my washing in the outside washing sinks and hung it up in the beautiful, peaceful garden, I was ready for afternoon tea served at 5 o'clock in the little patio which formed part of the out buildings. By this time several other pilgrims had arrived and we enjoyed pleasant camaraderie stimulated by real tea made in a tea pot! Round and round went the pot till empty only to be refilled by the gracious *hospitalera* , a lovely Scottish lady from Coatbridge in Lanarkshire. As we sat there in the warm sunshine, we were joined by one of the fathers from the adjacent Benedictine monastery. He was an amiable man with a warm affectionate nature, which immediately ingratiated him with us all. He poured himself a cup of tea and asked if anyone would be willing to read a Scripture passage at Evening Prayer of the Church at 7 o'clock. I immediately offered my services to read in English while a Dutch lady, Agnes would read in German and the knowledgeable English lady, Joyce, would read in French.

This would prove to be a thrilling event as we pilgrims who attended with the monks were joined by five sisters of the same order. Most of the service was carried out in Latin with Gregorian chant, which I did my best to follow, in a subdued bass/baritone. The tiny church was ancient, with an aura of history emanating from every stone. We readers did our duty well and I for one felt very at home. After the service, I and three of the women who had attended, went for a tasty meal and shared a bottle of wine in an old house which had been reconstructed and made into a restaurant. After the meal I returned to the church for Compline at half past nine. It was for me the realisation of boyhood fantasies intertwined with thoughts of the knights who protected the pilgrims on the road or went on to fight in the crusades. After Compline we received a Pilgrim's Blessing then I had my *credencial* stamped and retired very happy and at peace with world to dream of my Grail quest.

Approaching El Ganso – 15th April

El Ganso – typical Maragato village – the last
Moorish people in Spain – 15th April

Parish Church of Saint James – El Ganso – 15th April

The Refugio Gaucelmo – Rabanal – 15th April

Ruins of the Hospital San Juan outside Foncebadón – 16th April

La Cruz de Ferro 1504 metres above sea level
where pilgrims leave stones – 16th April

Near Punto Alto the highest point on the Camino Francais –
1515 metres – 16th April

The ancient streets of El Acebo de San Miguel – a Maragato
village – 16th April

The lovely haven of Riego de Ambrós – 16th April

16th Century Parish Church of Saint Mary Magdalen – Riego de Ambrós – 16th April

*Fellow pilgrim from Holland on the Bridge of the
Pilgrims – Molinaseca – 17th April*

The Knights Templar Castle – Ponferrada – 17th April

Tuesday 16ᵗʰ April 2013

People began stirring around 0615, the near-silent wraiths flitting purposefully from their beds to the facilities then back, to wrestle with sleeping bags, clothing and assorted paraphernalia in the subdued lighting of their own headlamps. Many of the lamps these days are thoughtfully tinted red which lends a Dante-esque feel to the ballet of pre-dawn preparations. I drift in and out of reality until the alarm of Agnes, the Dutch lady who lies adjacent to me, springs into life with a cheerful rendering of *"Eine kleine Nachtmusik "* on the dot of 0630. There are worse ways, I suppose, to be dragged from the embrace of Morpheus.

The hostel provided a light breakfast but I made my own porridge in the microwave from one of those handy sachets I had borne all the way from home. Microwaves in this context are excellent things in my opinion, because they procure time and convenience, and with Scotia's oats appropriately stowed away, down below, I was ready for the day.

Pilgrims were dissipating from 0730 onwards but I had still to arrange my bag's transport from the other albergue, Nuestra Señora de Pilar as I had done the previous day, for the albergue Gaucelmo had a policy of not handling bags. Again the *hospitalera* of N.S.de Pilar was most accommodating. I then set off and was soon passing everyone but the fastest. I felt strong and healthy, revelling in the sheer joy of the day which seemed to pulse bright and ozone clean, under an azure blue sky. In the distance the mountains stood out in clear relief, their tops still mantled in snow. At La Cruz de Ferro I caught up with an Irish girl we had dined with in Rabanal. This was quite an achievement for she was tall at five foot eleven and had a good stride. We took each other's photograph then walked together a while. I told her I could imagine her in a bright sunny place on the west of Ireland, hanging out the washing, with several healthy red headed children (for she had lovely red hair) running around her on the green grass. We spoke about Christ and as always I was at pains to convey the joy and wonder of His free gift of salvation. I find I frequently do this when I am speaking to folk who have been reared in the Catholic tradition, although the idea of "paying for our sins" and "working to gain entry to Heaven" is by no means unique to them.

The route led us through Foncebadón, La Cruz de Ferro, Monjardin, Punto Alto, El Acebo and Riego de Ambros. All of these villages are in parts decaying which fact inspired me to take many photographs. At almost every turn in the narrow streets there was a new view or some exciting detail of structure. Nowadays, strong efforts are being made to build the houses in the same vernacular style and some are very successful, although the recession has curtailed much of this activity.

I strode along with strength of a man of thirty five and would not have been anywhere else on earth. This was by far my best walking and I thanked God for it. When I reached Riego de Ambros, the albergue holding my gear was shut but I phoned the *hospitalero* who said he would let me in to collect it; then I booked into a *pensión* across the road and up the hill. It was a heavenly place set in its own grounds in which the lady owner was toiling at her plants which grew in great profusion and beauty. My room boasted a shower, toilet and a veranda from where I could see a little church beside which I had been told by my hostess there was a restaurant. I made my way there as soon as I was showered and ordered the ubiquitous *ensalada mixta* then returned to my veranda and dozed in the clear mountain air warmed by the friendly spring sunshine.

The English lady, Joyce, whom I had now encountered several times, eventually arrived and also booked herself into a room in the *pensión* being, unwilling to spend another night in communal lodgings. We agreed to eat together in the evening, when we were joined by a Dutch lady, Agnes, with whom we had now shared many miles of the Camino. Over dinner we noticed she was very subdued and it turned out she had wanted to leave a little pile of her recently deceased mother's ashes at La Cruz de Ferro, where there is a great mound of stones deposited over many years by pilgrims who had symbolically been relieved of some burden or other by their going on pilgrimage; she felt she could not do so when she saw someone behaving irreverently at the pile. I thought about her that night and prayed for her peace.

Incidentally the omelettes which we all had were really delicious.

Wednesday April 17th 2013

After a hearty breakfast of my own porridge, tea and toast, I set off around 0800 in the company of Joyce, who had spent the night at the same *pensión* as me, but said that I would walk at my own pace. She was very practical and encouraged me to forge ahead, so soon after taking some photographs of this lovely village I set off at a good lick enjoying the sheer exuberance of nature which was in a rapture of bud and promise, with endless clusters of plants vying for the most beautiful display. I had been going for about an hour when I overtook and fell in with Agnes, the lady from Holland who had been so down hearted at dinner. I listened to her sadness with great sympathy, simply wanting to provide a friendly ear. At length, when we had gone on for some time I said that I knew one thing for certain: that God loved her in Jesus

Christ and did not want her to be in this cast down condition. I told her that from the day I surrendered my life to Christ all things were radically changed for the better and that I became a new person no longer living for self but attempting always to live in the will of God. I could say that Christ had given me life and that more abundantly than I could ever have imagined.

She was very receptive and I thanked God, inwardly, for the privilege of speaking to her for she said that our talk had helped. We parted at Molinaseca, having taken each other's photograph by the bridge. I pushed on to Ponferrada via Campo and Mascarón and the iron bridge, which appears to be mostly made of stone, to view the Templar castle and the church of Basílica de la Encina where I prayed at the foot of a simple cross draped with a white cloth. I like simplicity and enjoy the peace of ancient spaces which have been places of prayer for a very long time. Like an oasis from the heat outside which even in April was intense for me, I was able to bring before God all those whom I had encountered on the trail, and shared with Him their needs and concerns. For me this is a large part of the "communion of the saints".

I then pressed on to the hotel Nova which, being close to the village of Columbrianos, stands right on the Camino and was all I could ask for. It is modern if you count the eighties as modern, and built in that aspirational style which did not envisage the economic troubles which would grip us towards the end of the first decade of the twenty first century. I soaked in a bath, washed my clothes and wrote my log noting from the pedometer I had only covered 17.4 kilometres that day. I filled in the time till dinner, which would not be available till 9 PM, by playing the chanter, planning the next day's journey and generally loafing around. Around 2030 I went into the bar lounge, a spacious and

The main Gate of the Castle - 17th April

*Basilica Santa
Maria de la Encina
– 17th April*

*Hotel Nova –
Ponferrada
– 17th April*

Iglesia de San Andreas – Ponferrada – 17th April

The Village of Cacabelos – 18th April

The Church in Cacabelos – 18th April

On the way to Villafranca – 18th April

The White House between the Pines – on the way to Villafranca – 18th April

The fertile country of El Bierzo – 18th April

Bridge over the Burbia into Villafranca del Bierzo – 18th April

airy space bereft, to my mind, of cosiness, and ordered an Estrella beer. This is one of my favourite beers, being just the right combination of lightness yet possessing the satisfying after-taste of heavier ale. By nine o'clock I was ready to eat the tablecloth and having migrated into the restaurant and ordered my meal, was at liberty to note that there were almost no women guests in the place! Suddenly the penny dropped that this was a hotel, albeit a very nice one, for men working on projects away from home. By 2200 I was getting weary and the shutters of my eyelids were coming down, so I succumbed and fell into a deep sleep. Sometime in the middle of the night I woke in a sweat for the room was hot. I opened the window and the noises of the night ushered me back to sleep.

Thursday 18th April 2013

I woke at the back of seven and after an invigorating shower, for I had sweated profusely overnight, made for the breakfast bar and stocked up on victuals with a croissant, tea, yogurt and orange juice. The orange juice in many of the cafes and bars is truly delicious and is produced by an ingenious machine which scoops up two oranges, simultaneously spigots them on two blades, squashes them and delivers the contents into the waiting glass. I could watch the process endlessly. On the road for eight o'clock and walking at about 4 kilometres per hour, I migrated steadily through Columbrianos, Fuentes Nuevas and Camponaraya. Almost every field and patch of land was being carefully prepared for sowing stimulating thoughts of home and my own allotment in Springburn which I knew would be lying like the bells that never rang. That is the price you pay, I suppose, when you throw over normality, the mundane and the regular, to embrace the spirit of the pilgrimage. That is why it works, I think.

There was not a thing I could do about what was going on at home and so my mind was liberated to focus on other things or nothing at all.

It is difficult to describe how fertile this land looks just now. Even the weeds are healthy and beautiful. The terrain becomes hillier as I press on westerly and so the acreage of vineyards increases. The vines are planted one and a half metres apart and appear to be set almost in straight lines although these wiggle comfortingly to resist regimentation.

There are woods before one reaches Cacabelos, and in these woods I came upon a German wood carver sitting on a stump and using a part of a tree trunk as his bench. I think I knew he was German as soon as I saw his tools for they were of exquisite manufacture and quality. His long black hair and beard would not have informed me of his ethnic origins. I engaged him in conversation and watched as he painstakingly shaved pieces of chestnut from the little block of wood he was working on. He was carving scallop shells for pilgrims, each one meticulously crafted with great skill and attention to detail. I was intrigued by his lifestyle and would have passed on after our chat without buying anything had I not noticed a beautiful cross of Santiago carved out of birch (I did not know it was this species until he told me) in the middle of his display of completed shells. The cross was hung by a beautiful and artfully fashioned leather thong made of multi-plaited thin strips of leather. I asked him how much it cost and he said 22 euros. I was slightly taken aback that the cross should be the same price as my steak back in Astorga; however, he explained that he had not made the leather necklace but relied on a colleague (who I sensed was female) and she had charged him 8 euros! So he said, and I had no reason to doubt him. So there and then in the forest before Cacabelos I purchased the first and probably the last cross I will ever wear. From that moment on I wore the cross every day on pilgrimage. After this interlude I pressed on for Cacabelos, where I visited the church, then on to Pieros, across the river Cúa, following the track as it veers away to the northward through yet more beautiful vineyards all being tended lovingly, very often by elderly people. I muse about whether or not the young are learning the skills of their grandparents. I suppose they must do for wine is big business in Spain. Today I notice the very first green shoots on the vines. When they prune the vines they leave two buds on each branch for the coming season's growth, and these are the shoots that are now bursting forth. By 1315 I was approaching Villafranca del Bierzo. It is a quaint village with the river Burbia running through it, and is set in the hollow of the glen. My lodgings for the night are on the west side of the bridge which crosses the river and are called the Albergue de la Piedra. After ablutions, I wrote my log in the Bar Burbia, noting I had walked 21.1 kilometres that day.

I met up with my Irish companion Diarmid, of a few days ago and we dined, (do I have to say I had hake?), in a recommended restaurant called Dom Natch, which was adequate without being outstanding, then returned to the albergue to enjoy a night which was mercifully quiet.

Friday 19th April 2013

I arose around seven and breakfasted on muesli, orange juice and tea. Diarmid and I then set off on what we thought was the road to the mountain but turned out to be the path which ran alongside the main road. These tarmacadam paths are referred to as *autopistas* for they are like tiny motorways for pilgrims. They are tough on the feet and often lead one through less inspiring country, always with the noise of traffic beside the pilgrim. This turn of events was very disappointing, for I had been looking forward to the climb since my heart and body felt so young after Rabanal. I even spurred myself at a great rate along the road, leaving my Irish friend behind to see if I could find a way onto the mountain path but there was none. It was in this rather disgruntled frame of mind, and after a brief debate with the Lord as to why this had happened, that I fell in with a lovely young woman whom we shall call Eve, from Vladivostok in Russia. She told me her parents had emigrated to Minnesota, although her accent still bore the strong pronunciations of a Russian speaker. It did not take long for us to move from the commonplace to more interesting conversation and I revealed to her how joyful I was feeling about my life in Christ. She immediately responded in like manner, revealing she had a strong faith in God but I suspected that she was willing, having spent some considerable time in India, to accept more than one way of salvation, although to be fair she spoke most of the time of Christ. I cannot compromise; for me Christ is all in all. I wondered, by the way she spoke of God being in all things, if she had realised that although all things consist by His word, He is not subject to His own creation, and is the Sovereign ruler of the universe.

We pressed on via Trabadelo, La Portela de Valcarce, Vega de Valcarce, and Rutelan, eventually arriving at Herrerias, to where I had arranged my bag be transported. My Russian companion decided to press on to La Faba, and I waved her farewell in that beautiful valley where the cow bells clanged with every movement of the cattle. Eventually Diarmid arrived and my bag was delivered. We then together, sought and found excellent rooms, with lovely facilities in Casa Herrerias. It would only cost me 10 euros, as I elected to use my sleeping bag. The sun shone brightly all day but there was a chill in the wind and I was glad of the bag that night.

After a shower I made my way to a bench beside the burn which ran through the village and wrote my log. The sun shone cheerfully without much heat but an air of peaceful abundance permeated the place which made it truly halcyon.

That night my Irish companion and I had a simple meal of Cuban rice followed by eggs, cheese and chips. It was adequate.

Saturday 20th April 2013

We rose around 0700 and breakfasted by 0740. Tea and toast do not take long to eat so we were on the road by 8 o'clock. Our way led through the valley following the river with little houses peppering the sides. Gradually the incline steepened and we were soon climbing through La Faba, Laguna de Castilla, onwards and upwards to O Cebreiro. My Irish friend and I conversed about many topics, often returning to the subject of Christ. The scandals which have plagued the Catholic Church in recent years have (possibly irreconcilably) driven away many who were perhaps never enamoured of the church , but strangely the true, simple Gospel is still recognised by searching souls and still changes lives forever.

At O Cebreiro we entered Galicia at an altitude of 1,330 metres with a wind which buffeted us apparently from every direction even on a relatively calm day, and doubtless it is for this reason the houses are built with wind-shunning shapes. The views were stunning in all directions and the little *pueblo* was made to feel quite jolly by the large numbers of tourists who, having been decanted from tour buses, wandered around taking photographs and buying souvenirs, with their cold weather gear on. Of course hardened pilgrims like us do not feel the cold!

From O Cebreiro we had one more, brief, steep climb to the highest point in the Galician Camino, and thanks to the Xunta of Galicia we can now count the kilometres falling away, for they have thoughtfully arranged for markers to be placed more or less every kilometre. I arrived at the albergue in Fonfría at half past two in the afternoon after a 21.5 kilometre hike to be pleasantly surprised by the construction of the place, which engendered a feeling of cosiness and reliability. I suppose one could describe the architecture as Galician-Alpine. The *literas* or communal sleeping area is built of un-squared wooden timbers as are the bunks, which creates a "rustic" look. This is the heart of the building. In reverse order, moving back out to the entrance, there is a warm and inviting sitting room where a Frenchman about my age is nursing very painful feet affected by tendonitis. I offer to let him use some of my "cure-all" cream from Frómista and he is most grateful. Next to the sitting room is a "roundhouse" which is a round wooden-clad room with a large central post supporting the roof timbers. This place is for donning and removing boots and packs. Then comes the bar, which is small but cheerful, selling the usual coffee, tea, beer and wines and spirits. Detached from the albergue, some fifty yards downhill is the restaurant, also built in the vernacular architecture of long ago, looking very like a Bronze or Iron Age roundhouse, with stone walls and thatched roof, which were common throughout Celtic Europe.

Dinner was ready by half past seven and we all, numbering about forty pilgrims made our way to the restaurant where we enjoyed a delicious three course meal for 10 euros. We started with spinach and bean soup with potatoes to give bulk. This was followed by a beef stew cooked with a lot of garlic, accompanied

8 AM Leaving Herrerías – frost and cowbells – 20th April

I climb into Galicia accompanied by a fellow pilgrim from Ireland – 20th April

Arriving at O'Cebriero – 20th April

Alto de San Roque altitude 1270 metres – 20th April

Iglesia de San Juan in Padornelo – 20th April

The bunkhouse in Albergue A Reboleira – Fonfria – 20th April

The restaurant at Albergue A Reboleira – Fonfria – 20th April

The restaurant of A Reboleira – separate from the albergue – 20th April

by boiled potatoes, and to finish off we had home-made Santiago cake, which is heavily flavoured with almonds. As always there was water and wine on the table. Many of the pilgrims were in party mood and were very cheerful. The table at which I sat was a little more subdued but populated with very interesting people. I sat beside the Dutch lady, Agnes, I had spoken to a couple of days ago, while opposite us was a Swiss chap in his forties I think, who had lost an arm. He had a strange desire to catch people off their guard, to disarm them, and when I spoke to him about this he said he liked to "pinch" them to make them "open up". I said there was no need for that for we were all "opening up" quite nicely and I was sure he was a lovely fellow underneath. Funnily enough when we came to the end of dinner Agnes gave me a sisterly peck on the cheek.

The *hospitaleira* and cook announced after dinner that there would be a "Celtic" ceremony whereby several bottles of various kinds of spirits were emptied into a chaffing dish and set on fire. The idea is to chase away evil spirits with the flames. I deemed myself to have been exorcised pretty well in the past so I forbore to taste it. I do not do well with spirits and might well have become the very embodiment of whatever demons they were trying to expel. When I arrived back at the albergue the husband of the *hospitaleira* had brought along his *gaita* or Galician bagpipe, for I had asked her if anyone played. So there and then we had an impromptu session. He was very skilful with Galician music, but their fingering is different to the Highland bagpipe and has to be learned, for our fingering renders several notes out of tune. However after a try I retrieved my chanter from the dormitory and we attempted to play together. Of course as the other pilgrims returned from the Celtic ceremony they had to hear us play and we had a brief, jolly interlude, but we were all exhausted and soon went to bed.

Sunday 21st April 2013

I was up and on the road for 0800 after breakfast. I said goodbye to my Irish companion for I was going to try to get to Sarria and he knew he would not. I had a delightful walk through Biduedo, Cruce, Triacastella, San Xil, Alto Riocabo, Furela, Pintin, and several other hamlets arriving at Sarria at 1430, with 28.4 kilometres on my pedometer. My overwhelming memory will be of the constant smell of dung and dairy cattle. These are not unpleasant smells and seem to impart to me a sense of well-being, and health. The area is so ripe and full of life I am unable to describe it. The flowers are blooming everywhere in vibrant colours and the weather which is cold with bright sunshine provides the perfect compliment.

I booked into the Alphonso IX hotel, because I have had enough of living cheek by jowl with others, although I will be back to an albergue tomorrow. I luxuriated in a bath and fancied myself a centurion coming off a long patrol; after all I had been marching along the Via Aquitania!

There is one aspect of the Camino which irks me and that is the lack of awareness of the Divinity and uniqueness of Christ which I come across time and time again. It is as though Jesus was just another good guy. For me this is far from the truth, for I believe Christ died for my sins and He alone is able to save me. It is one of many aspects of Christianity which set it apart from all other religions. It is that God purposefully takes the initiative and reaches out to sinners. I hope my book *"Water UnderThe Keel"* sells for it is the story of a man who loves Christ and Him alone.

The descent towards Triacastela – Islands in the mist – 21st April

Edible chestnut tree in the hamlet of Ramil – 21st April

The Chapel in the hamlet of As Pasantes – 21st April

The mist covered countryside between Triacastela and Sarria – 21st April

Sarria in sight – 21st April

One of the stone bridges which connect the Galician hamlets – 22nd April

100 Kilometres to go! I can hardly believe it – 22nd April

The dormitory in Albergue Ferramenteiro – Portomarín – 22nd April

View from the albergue patio – 22nd April

My bed in the Buen Camino Albergue – Palas de Rei – 23rd April

Octopus – very tasty and easy to share – a pulberia in Palas de Rei - 23rd April

Interior of San Tirso Parish Church – Palas de Rei – 23rd April

I had a delicious meal in the hotel consisting of fried pimentos followed by fried sea bream with a flan-type pastry for dessert. I did not leave the hotel after dinner but lay down till I fell asleep around half past ten, my head full of images and memories of the day. I can see big healthy cattle, lush, green pastureland and remember the smell of the dairy farms. These are strange things for me to contemplate before I sleep, but I suppose it is a measure of how disconnected I am from my normal life. I muse on whether or not I am being changed by the Camino, and admit that perhaps I am, although I realise I am still easily annoyed by what I consider to be stupidity. I drift into sleep admitting I am not a very tolerant man.

Monday 22nd April 2013

I rose at seven as usual and showered; I don't usually but it was such a lovely shower! My breakfast was paid for so I stocked up with a croissant, yogurt, fruit compote, and tea. Duly fortified in the inner man I set off through Sarria, which although picturesque in its own way is memorable for the steep ascent out of it. The route took me to Barbadelo, then through a whole series of tiny hamlets which more or less consisted of simply a collection of farm buildings on to Ferrerios, followed by yet more hamlets too many to name. The hamlets in the main seemed to coincide with kilometre markers which now faithfully appeared at their designated point and counted down the distance to my destination. I liked this and began to think of the end of the road. What is the end? Do I finish in Santiago or carry on to Finisterre? The countryside is unflinchingly beautiful, rich in its abundance. There are views to left and right which stimulate my sense of well-being and cause me to imagine scenes I hope to paint at home over the winter.

I arrive at my albergue where my extra sack is waiting, at around 1430. The hostel is immaculately clean and very large. With a name like Portomarin I would have expected it to be beside the sea but in fact it is perched above a man-made loch created for a hydro-electric project. In the bright sunshine the whole area looks idyllic, almost Mediterranean. I am bewildered by the variety of bird song in this vicinity, and, having showered and done my chores, I sit outside in the sun in a kind of reverie which can only be improved by a glass of cold beer. In order to fulfil my request, the *hospitaleira*, one of several, has to change the keg, but she is practised and efficient and in no time at all I am watching the droplets form on the glass she has placed on the my table overlooking the lake. I look around scarcely able to contain my sense of *joie de vivre* and on stealing a glance at the door in case anyone should witness the raptures of an older man who endeavours to convey an air of gravitas, am in time to witness the arrival of about forty young teenagers!

Peace is such a tender thing and often evaporates like thin fog in the morning. It comes and goes and if we are not quick to realise it we miss our chance to savour it.

This evening I dine with four English people and Lisa from Finland, with whom I have shared many miles from time to time. The four English folk whom I will now re-christen for the purposes of my little commentary are comprised of a lady, Joyce, I first met in Mazariffe, who texts me from time to time with good advice about albergues, Rodger, an ordained priest of the Anglican Church, Donald a chap in his middle forties who is about to start a course in evangelism, and Paul, a tall, thoughtful, introspective man of forty two years. The last three are friends and part of a small group pilgrimage. We enjoy an amiable, plain meal together and the conversation flows easily this way and that. I have home-made soup consisting of cabbage and potatoes, hake with a light lemony sauce, and Santiago cake with a satisfying flavour of almonds.

The day closes with a promise of good weather for the morrow which I confirm by accessing the German website Wetter3.de on the internet with my iPhone, only to be informed by that I am right enough and the weather should be fine up to the weekend, although I can see a cold snap coming around the end of the week. After dinner we return to our respective albergues and I wait for the return of the kids, who I find are from Madrid under the care of four teachers who assure me they are well behaved; and the children are fine as well! In fact there are forty two young folk of about fifteen or sixteen years. I turn in as usual at 10 PM whereupon the children return. They must have been exceptionally well behaved for I fell asleep immediately and did not stir till half past six.

Tuesday 23rd April 2013

People were dispersing from quite early on but I got away at 0730 travelling alone. Soon, as always seems to happen, I am overtaking people and I spy the tall thoughtful Englishman, Paul, up ahead. We remain with this distance between us for about an hour when he suddenly stops for a snack and I am able to catch up with him, whereupon we fall in together. He wants to keep our conversation clear of any personal revelations and is unwilling at first to venture beyond the superficial. I on the other hand, feeling myself so full of Christ's love for me and the realisation that He has a job for me on the Camino, am soon telling stories about my life at sea and my family that he begins to open up. He tells me he is trying to work out whether to get married to a lovely girl he has met. Having been married before he does not want to make another mistake. I cannot remember that time in my life so I am not sure if I can help him but I relate what I have. Around 1130 we stop at a little bar and I share my lunch. We are soon joined by Rodger the Anglican priest and we have a jolly time sitting eating my lunch in the sun. When we set off I walk with the priest and we make good speed for he is a strong walker, talking of the state of the universal church and the mission we have. Rodger is a kind man with great compassion and care for his little flock on the Camino. I feel sure that he would be the same for any flock he is put in charge of and I admire his faithful, caring heart. Like most Englishmen he is slow to drop his guard for fear of being hurt, but as the road falls away astern we realise that we serve the same Master and seek only His glory.

Our route had taken us through Gonzar, Ventas de Naron, Ligonde, and Eirexe, to Palas de Rei where we arrived at 1400, having averaged four kilometres per hour for six and a half hours. I had sent my bag to the albergue "Buen Camino" where I met up again with my companions, having been delayed a little when I visited a camera shop to find out how to operate a charger I had purchased earlier in the trip. I was a little ashamed when the lady in the camera shop initiated me into the secrets of my charger bought, I could not remember, how many leagues before. By 1500 I had showered, done my washing tended my feet, which were in excellent condition and began to write my log, in which I wrote "Life is good!" I had a beer in the shade of an umbrella in the plaza adjacent to the albergue and mulled over the day, absentmindedly tuning in from time to time to the conversations which bubbled up from several tables around me. At one table was a group of very attractive young French women who chatted away in animated fashion as they puffed in Gallic fashion, on the odd cigarette, whilst at another, a more mature group of men and women who may or may not have just met on the trail – I could not tell, laughed with each other as they conversed in a mixture of languages. When I closed my eyes and listened, these languages blended to a pleasant polyphony which lulled me into a soporific state until the hearty greeting of Rodger the Anglican priest as he sat down beside me, dragged me back to discourse and engagement with the present. We agreed to meet at 1830 for dinner whereupon he disappeared to attend to some pastoral duty for his tiny flock and I attempted with some success to return to my euphoria.

A *pulbereia* is a restaurant which specialises in octopus amongst other things. This is where we chose to eat, and this was an opportunity which I did not wish to miss, for I had noted several of these establishments on my walk and not yet succeeded in visiting one. I was dining with my three male companions from England so I ordered up a plate of octopus and shared it with them. I must say they took to it with great commitment even though they were first-timers and before long the plate was empty! Probably just as well for it can become slightly cloying in taste if one takes too much although there was no chance of that happening to me on this occasion. Not for the first time have I noticed how willing some fellows are to share my food! After this I had my customary hake which was by no means ordinary, for the taste was quite outstanding. We returned to the albergue by 10 PM. I had, in close proximity at the foot of my bed, an elderly Korean, who, spending most of the night on his back snored like a grampus accordingly. I am resolved that the joys of the albergue will be a special topic when I get home and relate this tale, for dormitory life for the more mature has limited appeal.

Wednesday 24ᵗʰ April 2013

I woke to the happy jingle of an iPhone belonging to one of two girls sleeping in my vicinity, adjacent to the snoring Korean. They had set the alarm for 0645 in case they slept in! I wonder what confused and turbulent state of mind can bring one to form the conclusion that an alarm will be necessary when only the brain dead and somnolent ancient Koreans can sleep through morning ablutions. Doors bang, taps run, toilets flush, Spaniards and Germans shout (they do not speak) and we are all called back to life and a new day.

I am up and breakfasted by 0730 and on the road accompanied by Donald the chap who is going to become an evangelist. He tells me his testimony and after listening carefully I am persuaded he has a calling to share his faith with others, and I resolve to pray that he will stay the course and prosper in his work.

Our road takes us through many hamlets too numerous to name, frequently leading us on paths which wander through fairly thick woods, and we make a good pace until we break for coffee at Furelos when we are joined by Rodger. When I go to the toilet they cast a cheery farewell and go on without me. I am glad, for I want to walk alone, however I soon I overhaul them because the aspirant evangelist has a bad knee which I try to alleviate with some magical Frómista ointment and wide Elastoplast. The rest of the day I spend alone, passing quickly through Melide, Boente, and Castaneda to arrive at the albergue Los Caminantes in Ribadiso at 1345. It is beautiful all respects with modern décor, lovely grassy areas which boast umbrellas and tables, and peace and quiet. I shower, do my washing and thank God for His goodness with the refrain of Psalm 136 going round in my head *"for His mercy endureth forever"* which, since it is repeated 36 times, is pretty emphatic. I have forty kilometres to go and I can hardly believe it!

At 1600, Eve, the lovely Russian girl to whom I had spoken some days ago, appeared. This was most unexpected for I thought she must have moved on. She is a very detached person in the way a cat is detached; nevertheless she seemed pleased to see me and gave me a hug in greeting.

I wrote my log in halcyon conditions under an umbrella, sipped a cold beer, and did a sketch of one of the rat-proof Galician store houses which was built to the rear of the albergue. Some these structures are very old and I have yet to see two which are identical. They are long and fairly narrow with pitched tiled roofs, constructed on raised stilts to prevent invasion by rodents in much the same way as the Romans did with their granaries.

As evening came on, a group of us assembled in the restaurant situated across the quiet country road from the hostel. Some had been my occasional travelling companions for quite a long time so it was a happy and convivial assembly. As usual I had what was now my staple diet, mixed salad, hake in some form or another, and crème caramel which the Spanish for some reason call "flan". I walked 24.5 kilometres today.

Thursday 25th April 2013

I rose at 0700 thanks to the alarm set by a nice Dutch girl, sleeping in the next tier of bunks to me. She belonged to a lovely family who were travelling with her, consisting of her father with whom I immediately found an affinity since he also had a "well used" face and had been around a bit, and two brothers who, having been well fed all their lives, towered over me, and their father, like giants.

I set off and walked all day with Paul. We had walked together before when he had shared with me his dilemma of what to do about marrying his girlfriend. He said that I had been able to help him make a decision about the rest of his life which was thrilling and very humbling. I do not believe I said anything particularly wise or uplifting but perhaps what I said enabled him to see more clearly what was in his own mind. Paul had been an architect but was now casting around for a new direction in which to point his life. He had carried out several commissions which had been successful and was very knowledgeable and sensitive to the needs of the human client as opposed to some "higher" ideal, which the critics will call fantastic and beautiful beyond words but which is actually completely impractical, cold and without feeling. We talked for some time about the vernacular architecture all around us and found much common ground. The road took us through Arzua then on through many other hamlets until we stopped at Salceda around 1100 for refreshments along with many other pilgrims. The Way was becoming very busy now, for many folk only walk the last one hundred kilometres from Sarria which allows them still to claim a "compostela". We pressed on to O Pedrouzo, arriving at 1345 with the temperature climbing rapidly towards being oppressive. I think I would not enjoy this walk in the height of summer.

The albergue called Otero was all that was needed, being modern, and clean with hot showers. How important simple things become! As the afternoon progressed it became very hot and having showered, attended to my working parts and done my washing, I may have allowed my eyelids to close for a short time.

*Leaving the Province of Lugo and entering the
Province of A Coruña – 24th April*

*The medieval Maria Magdelena Bridge over the
Rio Seco in Disicabo 24th April*

50 Kilometres to go – 24th April

West of Salceda 20 Kilometres to go – 25th April

The great Shell Altar – In the Church in O Pedrouzo – 25th April

The Church in O Pedrouzo – 25th April

*Santiago –
26th April*

*The Cathedral of
Santiago – 26th
April*

Hotel Pombal where I stayed in Santiago – 26th April

Side view of the Cathedral of Santiago – 26th April

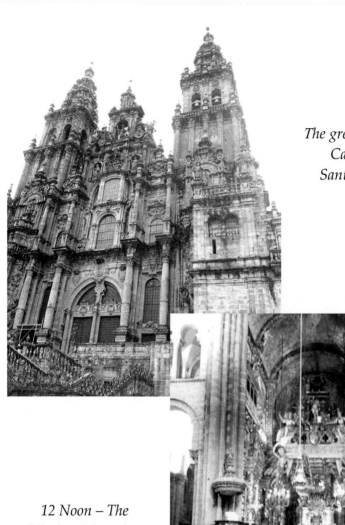

The great front of the Cathedral of Santiago – 26th April

12 Noon – The Pilgrims Mass then again at 7.30 PM with Botafumeiro 26th April

These brief naps are blissful interludes of oblivion, for both mind and body are worn out.

When I woke I sallied forth to look for the church. When I found it I noted the exterior was fairly plain despite a very ornate cupola; however on the inside it was quite breath-taking for behind the altar was a huge scallop shell about seventeen feet long and high, fashioned of plasterwork I think, with gilding which, being lit from behind made it all the more impressive. In the centre of the shell was a statue of Christ with His sacred heart. The statuary all around the church was understated and the more effective, I thought, for it. I stamped my pilgrim passport and found my English friends of the last few days. We searched around for a while and eventually found a restaurant which fitted the bill wherein I treated myself to tuna spaghetti, hake (of course) and flan (crème caramel – of course!) It was a most convivial meal at which I announced that I would walk alone tomorrow for the last day of my Camino, and Roger the priest announced that I should call my next book "Earth Under My Heel". I thought that was a sound idea. I suppose we were all in bed by 2200.

Friday 26th April 2013

After waking at 0200 I dozed off and on until the early birds started banging doors, snorting, running zips up and down, clicking, clunking and flushing from 0500 onwards. I saw the French, (including the chap whose foot had been treated by Frómista ointment), depart at 0530 in the dark, and lay until I could bear the on-going noise no longer. So I rose at six and made my own contribution to the cacophony. I was on the road by 0645 marching in the dark. I overheard two Uruguayan girls ahead of me who seemed to be lost in the dark so I put on my head-lamp and they followed me through the dark forest. They said I was their "star". I stayed with them till daylight then accelerated away. I apparently walk very quickly for a guy of my size and age. I really pushed the pace, stopping briefly at San Payo, where I engaged the lady owner of the bar in conversation. She was Spanish, but told me she had lived in England for a number of years. I asked if her return to Spain had been successful and she said that it had been the worst move of her life. In fact she said her life was ruined. Pretty strong words I thought but it just goes to show how hard the recession is biting. I then hot footed it to Santiago where I arrived at 1100. I went straight to the *Oficial Do Peregrino* to pick up my "Compostela" complete with Latin first name. They have difficulty converting Anglo-Saxon surnames. I was in time for the pilgrims' Mass and thankful that I had made it – it was thronged with people. My abiding memory of the whole service will be a nun in her autumn years who conducted the congregation in singing by using a method I had not seen since primary school. With outstretched right hand held in the horizontal plane she moved it up and down to steer us in the correct tonic direction. I refrained from joining in, even as I had done almost sixty years before.

After this I then found my way to the Hotel Pombal in the street of the same name and luxuriated in a hot bath. This was my kind of hotel, old fashioned, clean, quiet. sedate, well appointed. There is nothing quite as therapeutic as a hot bath after a rapid 20.5 kilometre hike, so I emerged much revitalised. I must have been very weary, for I kept lying down to revel in the joy of a clean bed, warm room and no people. How much, I now realise I value my own space! I flopped around for a long time and finally broke away from my lair to look at the city at 1700 as the shops opened. I looked around in vain for something to buy as "mindings" for the womenfolk at home, but most of the stuff on sale I thought looked pretty tatty. So I bought nothing. I circumnavigated the cathedral, taking the odd photograph and confirmed that they would swing the thurible (incense burner) at the 1930 Mass. For this reason I forbore to eat, with hunger pangs gnawing at my vitals.

I had first become aware of this event about fifty years ago in the Tivoli cinema in Partick in Glasgow. In between the films they would show interesting travel programmes which were called "Look at Life". I recall how the presenter had told a story about an occasion in the Middle Ages when the rope holding the incense burner had parted allowing the missile to hurtle through the door and kill a donkey out in the street! I have regaled family and friends with that story for years and now I am sure it is true, for the thurible, if it ever broke free it would cause carnage on a grand scale.

At 1900 I found a seat not far from the point of suspension of the thurible, with the church filling steadily, until by 1930, they were packing the aisles. The Mass was quite recognisable from the services I had witnessed elsewhere, as it should be, but they stand and sit at different times to Scottish Catholics. I tried to follow the bishop's sermon but it was hopeless. The highlight for me, the realisation of the desire formed in my youth, was the swinging of the thurible. The incense burner is suspended from a large pulley block set into the apex of an arch and fastened to the end of a long rope which divides into six ropes tails. Six burly robed helpers are each able to grasp a tail and begin by hoisting the burner up and down in short lifts until a pendulation starts. As the pendulum gains strength so the arc increases until it almost reaches the soaring arches at its highest trajectory. This was very, very impressive and a definite tick in my "bucket list".

I met up with my three English friends, exchanging greetings and farewells, then set a direct and solitary course for dinner, with distinct noises to challenge those produced by Humphrey Bogart in the film "African Queen" issuing from my stomach. I ate in a restaurant called Fornos.

For nineteen Euros I had four courses consisting of soup, scallops, steak and chips, café crème and tea, and of course water and wine. In addition to this, being placed near one of the corners of the restaurant, was again able to view discreetly my fellow diners (to my great amusement). People are wonderful! Replete, I returned to my hotel and slept like a corpse.

Saturday 27th April 2013

My plan had consolidated overnight and after a hearty breakfast at 0800, I jumped into a taxi to the bus station, and by 0900 was departing Santiago on a bus for Finisterre. The countryside as always is lush and fertile and eucalyptus trees, growing to well over 120 feet, abound in plantations. My heart leapt however, when I caught my first glimpse of the sea. I then realised what I had been missing for weeks – the sea! – I am a sea creature.

The bus sped safely round the not inconsiderable bends along this delightful coastline and my awareness of the recession, which has hurt so much of Spain, was re-kindled only by the sight of the odd uncompleted housing project. Otherwise life looked pretty good.

My fellow passengers and I decanted at Finisterre at 1100 and I made my way as quickly as I could to the Cape to see the lighthouse and the sea. It was thrilling to gulp in the clean salt air, watch the low swell forming offshore and trace its inexorable drive to the rocks where it crashed and foamed into spume and spindrift.

The scene was beautiful and impressive but no more so than our own mighty headlands in Scotland or Ireland. And with this thought I pondered the ancient trade which was carried out from prehistoric times along these coastlands, all the way to distant Hibernia and Britannia. I mused about the connective power of the sea as it laves every continent of the globe, and how, above all tangible elements it is the one that not only gives us life but joins us one continent to another.

I dutifully photographed the lighthouse, the sea, the sky, the surf and anything else I could imagine Patsy chivvying me about. I am not a photographer. I have admitted this before but my shortcomings were forcibly brought home to me as I observed, from my nesting sight, like a large gannet having a picnic, a "real" photographer at work. With equipment costing many thousands of pounds he set about positioning his camera at just the correct correlation with the rays of the sun; skilfully gauging the shadow-transit of the marram grass, and peering with great patience into the lens, until, at just the right moment, he took the shot - of a brass name plate which reassured all of us that we were, in fact, at Finisterre! Actually I have forgotten what the plaque said but it must have been important.

In the shop on the Cape I was able to purchase in 5 minutes the "mindings" for the womenfolk I had agonised over the night before. These turned out to be porcelain medallions each secured by a leather thong, with a unique Celtic design signifying some emotion or quality like love, or faithfulness, or fruitfulness. I then began to make my way back, being quite prepared to walk to the relative civilization of the village of Cee, for my concept of distance had, and remains, altered. I am now quite happy to contemplate a long march, but the rogue thought sprang up that I could ask the driver of a Saga tours bus if I could hitch a ride to Cee then change buses to Muxía. He agreed and picked me up about a kilometre down the road when he had rounded up his flock. As I boarded I was met by quizzical geriatric stares and as I was about to explain myself, the lovely tour guide, a young woman in her twenties, announced over the sound system who I was and explained my walk. This was met with loud cheers and clapping so that I felt quite heroic for a second or two.

I was soon in Cee and, having thanked my kind driver and his lovely assistant profusely, went to the station to find I had missed the last bus by some four hours, so I hired a taxi to take me to Muxía, via my hotel for the night, which Patsy had organised for me. On arriving at my hotel I was met by Carmen the owner, who discharged my taxi and undertook not only to take me to Muxía but also to retrieve me when I had finished sightseeing. The village is pretty but has a modern feel which I was not expecting; however I wandered around taking photographs, being particularly taken by the ship models in the church of Virgen de la Barca.

As I say, we had agreed that Carmen should come and collect me around 5 PM from the BAR O PORTO, where I had fetched up after my tour of the environs. I liked this bar. It was a seaman's place with memorabilia of the sea all around and photographs of old fishing boats. I had about an hour to kill before my lift would arrive so I started to chat to an attractive lady who was perched on a stool along from me at the bar. It turned out she owned the place and we prattled away happily in Spanish, which bore testimony to her patience and measured pace of speech. It was a pleasant diversion until my lift arrived just before five.

*Finisterre Lighthouse
– 27th April*

*Muxia fishing village
– 27th April*

*Ship models in the
Church Virgen de la
Barca – Muxia – 27th
April*

Captain David Littlejohn Beveridge

The lower light at Finisterre – 27ᵗʰ April

Tourino Faro – The real end of the earth. – 27th April

Down at the surf beach Nivena – photo taken by Carmen the hotel owner
– 27th April

The edge of the sea – 27th April

Lounge in Hotel Fontequeirso – 27th April

Casa Fontequeirso – Carmen's hotel – 27th April

Carmen, my host and driver, insisted that we visit the "real" Finisterre at Torino Faro where there is a small cylindrical light house, (Position: 42 degrees 52 minutes 52 seconds North 09 degrees 16 minutes 18 seconds West, thanks to iPhone) and the beach at Niveña. This is a surf beach favoured by the doyens of the sport and I watched fascinated, as they skilfully rode the combers.

On my return to the hotel I showered in a delightful cabinet which boasted many heads producing hot therapeutic water from all directions at the turn of a valve. For the true pilgrim this is sheer hedonism but frankly I could not have cared less. Hot water is a wonderful gift, and when it comes in controllable fountains of invigorating pleasure I am happy to find myself in the camp of the hedonists.

Carmen cooked my delicious fish dinner and, sitting alone, I ate it in her comfortable dining room. The fish was followed by the now inevitable café crème which had become part of my staple diet, having consumed the dish almost every night on my journey. I am not complaining; I still enjoy it!

I could hear Carmen working away at her scullery sink listening to Basque music. I commented on how much I enjoyed it when she returned and offered to make coffee. I agreed immediately for Spanish coffee, even the decaffeinated variety, as I mentioned before, is not to be avoided. She returned with a tray and I invited her to sit down and share a cup as we were the only souls in the hotel. She asked me about my life, so in a mixture of English, Spanish and German (for she had lived for some time there) I did my best to tell my story ending with my faith in Christ Jesus. She was very impressed by this for the poor girl had been under great stress with one thing and another and I tried to help her to understand that Jesus had the answers to all her troubles.

After this I went for a walk, spoke to Patsy and turned in to sleep well in the quiet of the countryside.

Sunday 28th April 2013

I woke at 0630 and was breakfasting at five to seven. Carmen insisted on and produced tea and toast which I devoured. We set off at 0713 to drive 15 kilometres to Muxía. The roads are winding and twisting. It was dawn and a low mist hung over the valleys. She drove as one possessed, throwing the car around corners with great verve and determination. I was not uncomfortable and indeed inwardly encouraged her for I would have done anything not to miss the bus. In the event we made it with six minutes to spare. Carmen gave me a Continental kiss on each cheek and tore into the advancing morning with my heartfelt thanks ringing in her ears. I caught the bus along with several other pilgrims and we set off at about 0740, arriving in Santiago at 1000. By the time I arrived in the Hotel Pombal again I had decided to go home by ship from Santander on the morrow. This involved a significant amount of work on the computer which I would not have managed without the help of the concierge (another Carmen). At the same time Patsy was working her socks off arranging things from home. I took lunch at 1300 in Santiago then rested till it was time to leave for the bus station by taxi.

We left in a lovely Bosch bus at 1800 promptly. The bus was not new but it was well maintained with many modern conveniences like "climate control" and movies. We changed drivers 3 times as we steadily made our way from Santiago to A Coruña with the sky gradually darkening as evening came on. In the dark I lost track of time and space and existed only in the little bubble of our time machine. I had never been in a bus for such a long time but the journey was made easier by the Spaniards and Gallegos who adhere to the seats they are given and do not as a rule invade each other's space. The descent from the mountains was both interesting and exhilarating, involving skilful driving to negotiate the many hairpin bends. I could see the headlines "Aging Scots pilgrim walks 800 kilometres on the Way of St. James - dies in auto-bus crash". I confess inwardly to well-developed dour streak which has taken a lifetime to perfect.

Monday 29th April 2013

My seat mate changed around 2 AM and the woman who had maintained an aloof silence for the entire journey was replaced by a man who snored, open-mouthed, loudly and interminably. I am becoming more tolerant and I just thole it (Scots and perhaps Old English word- means to put up with). At last, around a quarter to four in the morning we reach Santander and I alight from the bus with that sense of disorientation which always accompanies early morning arrivals. My destination, thanks to Patsy's tremendous efforts is the Hostel Liebena. Despite her clear instructions on how to get there, I chicken out and take a taxi which dumps me at the door three minutes after leaving the station. The frontage of the hostel is in darkness but the door is open. A single candle illuminates the stairwell, and while I appreciate romantic ambience as much as the next man I feel this may be a step too far. I grope upstairs with my huge rucksack which is back to maximum loading and find the desk. There are two male watchmen sharing another candle in a saucer. To my Camino-suffused mind they are like monks copying out the Scriptures. The older, unshaven one, who appears to have Romany blood in him, explains there is a power cut but it will be back on by 0700! This is only 3 hours away so it does not bother me too much, particularly when I am handed my own candle in a tiny storm lantern. These are reserved for guests – staff members only get saucers. My unshaven gypsy shows me to my room and it is clean (as far as I can tell by candlelight) and well appointed. It only lacks modern lighting. My host tests the hot water and declares it "OK" with an ambivalent shake of the head, indicating something deeply Iberian and mystical. I am happy to clean my teeth and fall into bed between the sheets. I am cold and wake after two hours. I leap from bed and dig out my silk sleeping bag liner, refusing to resort to the sleeping bag in these salubrious surroundings. Things improve with the liner and my fleece over my torso and I sleep for another couple of hours. I am awakened by the loud noise of the street as the re-cycling lorry picks up three large loads of bottles. There is an orgy of breaking glass lasting several minutes and I resolve to suggest double glazing to the gypsy in the morning. When I rise to dress at 0900 I discover the window has been open all night! I often astonish myself with how thick and slow I am and this is one of these occasions.

By 1000 I eat my fruit and the last piece of sheep's cheese, a relic from my walk retained for emergencies. I know it is sheep's cheese because Carmen the hotel owner told me so. It is apparently very nourishing and keeps quite well.

My gypsy friend, for we are now friends after the shared experience of our nocturnal meanderings, says I can leave my gear in the room, so I strike out to investigate my surroundings. After a couple of abortive attempts I find the offices of Brittany Ferries and the kind lady behind the desk not only assures me I have paid everything but also issues me with a boarding pass. Things are improving. With an air of growing confidence I cross the road and order an omelette and bacon in a bistro. Delicious and fortifying!

I decide, on advice from Brittany Ferry lady, that I need a small sack for personal effects on the ship as my bag can be locked away in the baggage locker. I find the very thing for 7 Euros and return to my room to decide on its contents. By 1230 I am ready to leave Spain, but Spain will not let me go as I cannot board till 1415 Spanish time. I decide I need salad and visit another bistro which also attracts dog owners who possess exotic dogs. One looks like a living mop, another like a black West Highland terrier with long legs, sporting a red bow tie.

This will be my last *ensalada mixta* for this trip, I am glad to say, and I leave the bistro feeling superior and healthy and hungry. The superannuated paunch which had been creeping up on me prior to my walk has largely disappeared so much so that my belt is unable, with the present number of holes to cope with my slim frame. I contemplate just using my knife to make a hole then, as by magic, I come upon a garage where the mechanic is both willing and able to punch a new hole with a purpose made punch.

The *PONT-AVEN* is enormous. I am used to ships and she *is* enormous. She has ten decks with wonderful facilities which make our little ferries to Ireland and the islands look small and shabby. With several restaurants and cafeteria, bars of differing ambiance, live entertainment, featuring singers, comperes running quizzes and even a piano player, it is able to provide for just about every taste. I must say it is very cheerful and has the feel of what I imagine a cruise liner is like, for I never have and never will sail on one if I can help it.

We sail at 1445 Spanish time and her mighty thrusters lift her effortlessly off the quay and in to the channel. The sea is mercifully calm to start with and I hope it remains so. I am six years away from the sea and don't want to make a fool of myself. As we make our way out into the Bay of Biscay I realise afresh that

I could not go cruising. The whole idea causes me to cringe. My sea-going involved being busy and doing something useful. For me this is indolent and time wasting. I suppose that's just me. I have dinner and contrary to my earlier resolution I have yet another mixed salad followed by baked cod and tarragon sauce. That in turn was rounded off by a lemon-type yogurt. It was very tasty but that is definitely the last *ensalada mixta* for a while. I buy a book by Clive Cussler called "The Tombs", and read it till bedtime, then repair to the "Quiet Lounge" where I have reserved a reclining seat. It is quiet except for the snoring and whispering which are both very loud! At 2300 the steward mercifully extinguishes the light except for the emergency exit which glows green and malevolent above my head, bestowing a luminous aura over the recumbent passengers, like so many corpses in a morgue. I decide to retrieve my sleeping bag from the luggage locker and lie on the deck where I can more easily study the Emergency Exit sign. Sleep eventually overtakes me as I lie and listen to the familiar throb and pulse of a ship at sea; remembering when I was in charge and *so* in tune with my ship that every nuance of her passage through the sea was a message to me. I sleep fairly soundly till about 0400, only repositioning myself to avoid the several contents of my trousers which have become my pillow. I rise to avail myself of the facilities and notice Ushant lighthouse on the port beam, noting that, on the GPS-driven chart, which anyone can see, the speed is down to 16 knots. Automatically I calculate we are running into seven knots of tide because the moon is full and it is the time of Spring tides.

Tuesday 30th April 2013

I rise at six and with albergue-trained skill silently extricate myself from the womb of my bag, stuff it into its sack and set about buying a shower pack, containing shampoo, soap and a towel, all for £3.40. As always, I say *always*, the shower head is a challenge and I narrowly miss soaking my clothes with its wild thrashing around when I turn it on. The water, however, is mercifully hot and refreshing so duly cleansed and doused in Old Spice I am ready for breakfast. I am determined to eat healthily so I select everything I think is healthy and end up taking on over 1000 calories! (I comfort myself that I am still recovering from the walk and can still use the new hole in my belt). After breakfast I ask if I can see the bridge, playing on my status as ancient mariner, and am given permission, after six phone calls by the Information Desk, to present myself at 1000 to be escorted to the Bridge. I am thankful. I fill in the time till then walking on deck, on top of the Wheelhouse in 30 knots of wind. This plus the 23 knots of the *PONT-AVEN* comes to 53 knots – just under a healthy bracing force 10!

I am ready for the Bridge at 0940, and after a further 4 phone calls am led there by the charming Magli. In her late twenties, she is a kind of general factotum possessing a rank I am unfamiliar with. She is friendly and pretty and I enjoy the journey to the Bridge, where entering the after door felt like coming home to the *JURA*. All her gear was the same and I could easily have stood a watch there. The officers are charming and after a few minutes the Old Man appears and we chat. I do not overstay my welcome for I know the feelings. I am happy and ready for a coffee, sure that we are in safe hands.

After coffee and a raisin cake which is actually a Chelsea bun posing as a healthy option, I sit down to read, enjoying the simple language and plot of Cussler's latest collaboration. He must be very old now but I admire the way he continues to produce his yarns. The sceptic in me wonders if he is still alive; I hope he is for he has often whiled away an hour or two for me. After a spell of this I decide to move forward to see if the sea has changed much as we head further up the English Channel. I am not being facetious, seamen watch the sea all the time.

As I pass I am hailed by Trevor and Ann, a lovely couple from Derbyshire whom I first met in the departure lounge. Trevor wants to talk and we have a pleasant conversation which lasts till we reach Portsmouth! Amazing how the time goes, in pleasant company. We arrive exactly on time at 1415 and I am impressed by the efficiency of the ship and her crew. There is a bus driven by a Scotsman, who is so pleased to meet a fellow countryman that when I ask if can make my train time, he assures me he will get me to Aberdeen on time if need be! Such is the loneliness of the expatriate Scot. I only want to go to Portsmouth station so he is as good as his word and we arrive in plenty of time for the train, which I board with a growing sense of being on home ground. After a couple of stops I start up a conversation with a young man in a business suit and sneakers from Manchester. His feet are sore because of his new shoes as he has been to an interview for a new job. I tell him stories of the Camino – he is amused and resolved no longer to bother about his feet - we are friends. We part in Waterloo and he tells me how to get to Euston. The tube is relentlessly efficient and I am soon on the concourse one hour ahead of schedule asking the nice ticket collector if it is in order to take the earlier train. He assures me with an enthusiasm that I thought had departed with the Fifties that it is. I am soon travelling at well over 100 mph and I buy an Aberdeen Angus beef-burger, some wine which allegedly comes from the Rioja region, and apple yogurt. It is good to be on home ground and suddenly I realise my Camino is ending.

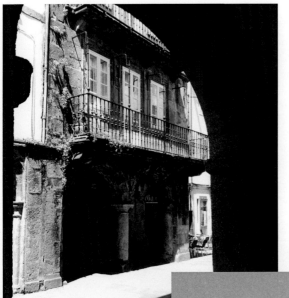

Back to Santiago for 10 AM – 28th April

A last shot in front of the Cathedral before departing for Santander 28th April

*Ensalada Mixta
– 29th April*

4 AM arrival and power cut in Hostel Liebena - 29th April

The Pont Aven - 29th April

Portsmouth and HMS Warrior – 30th April

I am not sorry. Not really. I have had the journey of a lifetime and several people, knowing what I have done, have already shaken my hand and said "We salute you, sir". (I probably look older than I am so that's OK). We race towards Scotland and the love of my wife and family and the responsibilities of life, and yet somewhere in the back of my mind is a still, small voice asking the question "I wonder what the Camino Portugués is like?"

Great to be back! 30th April

EPILOGUE

A year and more has come and gone since I walked across Spain on the Camino de Santiago. Time enough, I say, to reflect and place in context my experiences.

When I first resolved to make the journey I was intent on fulfilling a vague dream and aspiration from my youth. I was not seeking redemption, forgiveness, or the reconciliation of life problems. The first two were long since dealt with when I trusted forever, in the saving power of the shed blood of Christ; the third is the common lot of mankind, and so we have all to struggle through as best we can, with or without faith.

There is nothing magical about the Camino de Santiago. It does not of itself, either by its length, rigour or the places it passes through solve anything in my view. What it does do, and this may well contain a mystical dimension, is to permit in very subtle ways, human beings to interact and share parts of their lives with candour and at a deeper level than they might ordinarily ever do. There is something unifying about the common experience of daily toil on a single road which must be traversed, sometimes in company, whether we like it or not. We are obliged to interact with one another and out of this; we form bonds be they never so ephemeral and transient. We offer opinions; a sounding board, another point of view, and sometimes, a word in season; a word which actually helps a fellow pilgrim.

It took about ten days for me to realise, quite suddenly, having been asked many times why I was on the Way of St. James, that I might have something to give rather than to receive. After all I find it easy to talk to people and the fact that I look old and have a "lived in" face, may well cause folk to think I have some experience to pass on. From that moment on my pilgrimage became much more valuable to me and endowed the enterprise with a sense of purpose it had not hitherto possessed. I eagerly looked forward each day to the encounters that might lie ahead and the opportunities I might be afforded to tell others about Jesus. I have to say this altered perspective not only filled my pilgrimage with new purpose but it continues to this day. I have been changed and enriched. That is not all. I became aware and continue to be aware, that I have been, all my life, less than tolerant of my fellow human beings. That facet of my character has been altered, I think for the better. There is nothing like a spell of life in the albergues of the camino not only to highlight the merits of our accompanying life-travellers but also to school us in the art of "live and let live".

Each day since returning home I have remembered the Camino de Santiago. I remember long, bone weary days, strong wind, driving rain, hot sun, the joy of day's end and the fellowship of good companions. It haunts my mind and inspires my art, and it calls to me irresistibly, so that soon, if I am spared, I will be a pilgrim again.

Also by the Same Author

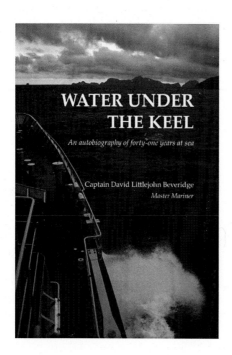

Born in the ancient fishing village of Rosehearty on the Moray Firth coast in 1949, David Littlejohn Beveridge went to sea in June 1966 as a deck apprentice with T & J Brocklebank.
In 1978 he joined the Department of Agriculture and Fisheries for Scotland (later the Scottish Fisheries Protection Agency), achieving command in 1987.
Water Under the Keel is his autobiography.

Paperback ISBN: 9781780355672
Kindle ISBN: 9781780359752
e-Pub ISBN: 9781780359745

Available from
http://www.fast-print.net/bookshop/1280/water-under-the-keel